CYRANO AND MOLIÈRE

Borgo Press Books by FRANK J. MORLOCK

The Chevalier d'Éon and Other Short Farces from the Eighteenth- and Nineteenth-Century French Theatre (Editor)
Chuzzlewit
Congreve's Comedy of Manners
Crime and Punishment
Cyrano and Molière: Five Plays by or About Molière (Editor)
Falstaff (with William Shakespeare, John Dennis, and William Kendrick)
Fathers and Sons
The Idiot
Jurgen
Justine
Lord Jim
Notes from the Underground
Oblomov
Old Creole Days
Outrageous Women: Lady Macbeth and Other French Plays (editor and translator)
Peter and Alexis
The Princess Casamassima
A Raw Youth
The Stendhal Hamlet Scenarios and Other Shakespearean Shorts from the French (editor and translator)
Two Voltairean Plays: The Triumvirate and Comedy at Ferney (editor)
The Widow's Husband; and, Porthos in Search of an Outfit: Two Dumasian Comedies (editor and translator)

CYRANO AND MOLIÈRE

FIVE PLAYS BY OR ABOUT MOLIÈRE

FRANK J. MORLOCK,

EDITOR

THE BORGO PRESS
MMXIII

CYRANO AND MOLIÈRE

Copyright © 2001, 2004, 2013 by Frank J. Morlock

FIRST EDITION

Published by Wildside Press LLC

www.wildsidebooks.com

DEDICATION

For María del Carmen Martínez Sánchez

CONTENTS

MOLIÈRE AT NINON'S; OR, THE READING OF TARTUFFE, by René de Chazet and Jean-Baptiste Dubois. 9
CAST OF CHARACTERS 10
MOLIÈRE AT NINON'S (text) 12
SCENE ADDED FOR THE ANNIVERSARY OF MOLIÈRE, by Charles-François-Jean-Baptiste Moreau 77
CAST OF CHARACTERS. 78
SCENE ADDED FOR THE ANNIVERSARY OF MOLIÈRE (text). 79
THE KING IS WAITING, by George Sand 93
CAST OF CHARACTERS. 94
THE KING IS WAITING (text) 96
CYRANO AND MOLIÈRE, by George Jubin. 123
TRANSLATOR'S NOTE. 124
CAST OF CHARACTERS. 126
CYRANO AND MOLIÈRE (text) 127

THE LOVE DOCTOR, by Molière 161

CAST OF CHARACTERS 162

PROLOGUE (text) 164

ACT I 166

ACT II 183

ACT III 200

ABOUT THE AUTHOR 220

MOLIÈRE AT NINON'S
OR, THE READING OF TARTUFFE, by René de Chazet and Jean-Baptiste Dubois

CAST OF CHARACTERS

MOLIÈRE

NINON

PRINCE DE CONDÉ

PIERRE CORNEILLE

RACINE

BOILEAU

LA FONTAINE

CHAPELLE

SAINT-ALBAN, Secretary to the President

LAFORET, Molière's servant woman

A PAGE

TWO LORDS

A VALET

MOLIÈRE AT NINON'S

The action takes place in a room belonging to Ninon de l'Enclos.

CHAPELLE:

Gentlemen, in a moment you are going to see Ninon.

A LORD:

You seem very emotional.

CHAPELLE:

I am.

A LORD:

Everything is fine!

CHAPELLE:

You don't guess?

A LORD:

Why, I think I understand you.

Ninon has seduced you.

CHAPELLE:

I cannot protect myself against it

I placed my life's happiness under her sway.

Her face, a look, just the sound of her voice

All charm me, animate me, and bring to my soul

The guilty embarrassment of a secret passion.

A LORD:

Isn't Chapelle astonished by his love

He whose heart never burned for more than a day?

CHAPELLE:

Well, Ninon, I think has changed my character.

Firm in friendship, capricious in her loves

I find an invincible attraction in adoring her;

To please is her habit, and to charm is her secret.

As for wit, what a woman! Around her ceaselessly,

Talent, genius—bustles, soars, and surges.

A scholar without pride, a beauty without vanity

Everything is perfection in her, and nothing is borrowed.

She knows how to attract, grace has doubled her arsenal.

Friends for her heart, lovers for her charms

In a word, beauty, wit and reason.

You see everything joined together when you see Ninon

Here she comes.

NINON: (entering)

Pardon if I am unable to give myself—

CHAPELLE:

When hope sustains us, we can wait without pain.

NINON:

Gentlemen, I have some plans for you this evening.

CHAPELLE:

What plans? Madame, ah, dispose of us.

NINON:

Are you free?

A LORD:

Why—

NINON:

Come on, be frank. What gallant scheme?

A LORD:

If I must tell. A certain rendezvous.

NINON:

You'll be there?

A LORD:

Indeed, yes.

NINON: (smiling)

Indeed, you won't.

A LORD:

Why not?

NINON:

You are going to put it off.

A LORD:

We really promised.

NINON:

To fail in one's promise in love is a game. False delicacy!

I can count on you tonight, right?

You are hesitating—Truly—You are whispering?

CHAPELLE:

Can one resist you?

NINON:

Eh, great gods! how much trouble!

I'm only enchaining you for tonight, gentlemen.

CHAPELLE:

Let it be for life!

NINON:

Ah! Fine sentiment!

For life! finish up? Quickly take an oath

Give me the assurance of an eternal love;

As for me I will swear to you an equal constancy,

We will lie together. But this is very discursive;

Know then why I want to keep you.

This evening they are giving a fine work at the theatre

Whose purpose is moral, whose tone is true, and whose plan is wise,

Whose characters are all new and well delineated.

In a word, a work that is well written, well thought out.

We owe this masterpiece to that clever author

True in all his scenes, natural in his style

Whose bold grace and frank gaiety

Are the sacred titles of immortality.

You recognize him, right?

ALL:

It's Molière.

NINON:

Tonight his Tartuffe is submitted to the pit.

Now that's why Ninon wants to enchain you.

Well, will you allow yourself to be easily dragged along?

You leave love without regret for genius.

And sad passions for a comedy

There's always time to utter a sigh,

And there's never leisure for a masterpiece.

Indeed, if twenty beauties flatter your hopes

You have only Molière to celebrate in France.

Come, come tonight—You know, my friends,

That this illustrious author has many enemies

Even at court; it's necessary, united by his victory,

By common efforts, to favor his glory.

Trust me: by protecting the flight of Tartuffe

We are protecting a treasure for posterity.

VALET: (entering)

Mr. de Saint-Alban.

NINON:

Molière's enemy!

CHAPELLE:

Eh, what! the odious secretary of the president!

NINON: (uneasy)

I wasn't expecting him and I tremble.

CHAPELLE:

What!

NINON:

This man who feigns a zeal so fervent

Is a holy impostor whose visit conceals

A disturbing purpose. You know that he is determined

To ruin Molière in the mind

Of the first President, and is a powerful enemy of Tartuffe.

I hear him. You will know all he's going to tell me;

Tonight, at the theatre, be sure to remember to be there.

CHAPELLE:

Yes, Ninon:

To see Tartuffe and bow to your wishes

Instead of a single pleasure, that's to encounter two.

(He leaves with the lords. After they have gone, Saint-Alban enters.)

SAINT-ALBAN:

An important motive leads me to you, Madam.

NINON:

I believe it, would you take the trouble—

SAINT-ALBAN:

No, madam, two words and I am leaving momentarily.

In you Molière finds constant support

They told me?

NINON:

It's true.

SAINT-ALBAN:

You admit it without fear.

NINON:

Molière is my friend; I say it again without subterfuge.

SAINT-ALBAN:

What a friend! do you know what odious conspiracy

He's inventing to deceive all eyes today?

NINON:

I am unaware of everything; speak.

SAINT-ALBAN:

In confidence, I am

Going to reveal to you this conspiracy; of your trust

You will see that this man is forever unworthy.

NINON:

Why, sir, are you going to speak?

SAINT-ALBAN:

Know these crimes.

You know that he's spreading it about that our great monarch

Who, for once too weak, giving him marks

Of mad friendship, is formally permitting

Them to represent Tartuffe in Paris.

NINON:

Well?

SAINT-ALBAN:

He's lying.

Myself as well as you, I fell into the trap.

But at last I know his criminal plot.

They write me just now by the courier from Lille

That the work is forbidden by the king, proscribed.

You see what trick Molière was capable of.

Stop receiving such a guilty man

Who to better insult the supporters of the faith

Dares to disguise the will of the king from us.

NINON:

No, sir, I know and esteem Molière

They want to ruin him but the ruse is very clumsy.

The order is true, actually given, Tartuffe is allowed.

But this order is verbal; evil enemies

Are revoking it by doubting and refusing to believe it.

Molière is innocent, I love him and I glory in it.

Here at my home, you will see him whatever the weather.

I admire his goodness, his virtues, his talents.

SAINT-ALBAN:

His goodness! When his pen wounds and shreds:

His virtues! When his heart sighs for a thousand female charms

His talents!

NINON:

That's enough; they are known everywhere.

So, let's speak rather of his pretended faults.

Where can you find them in Tartuffe?

SAINT-ALBAN:

Where can I find them? Gods! Why must you be instructed?

Against true believers, his darts and his bon-mots.

NINON:

You are deceiving yourself: far from attacking the devout,

He's offering his genius to religion

To arm reason against hypocrisy.

Saint-Alban, return to your unjust mistake:

Judge better of Molière and especially his heart.

Beware of imitating this crowd of fools

Who want to kill the mind and enslave thought.

Understand Molière and guide him and support him

Let, his work play today,

And think that everywhere justly he is renowned

Who is the protector of a great man.

SAINT-ALBAN:

No, Madame, Tartuffe is a child still born

Which, from this day, must be condémned to be forgotten

The President wishes it: your passionate prayer,

That of courtiers and all of France

Won't make me bend: Tartuffe is in its tomb.

NINON:

You believe that? Its success won't be less grand

Vainly you want it to die, to be forgotten;

As for me, I will do everything to make it live.

Yes, I intend to give it a deserved fame

In all weather I've counted on illustrious friends.

I am going to assemble them, and in an immense club

That can be called the elite of France

Molière will come to read this immortal work

With relish, that intrigue scorns.

SAINT-ALBAN:

What?

NINON:

To gather them, I am rushing to write them,

To come here, tonight, and you will hear Molière read.

For a stage, he will have this salon

And Tartuffe will have been played at Ninon's.

(Exit Ninon.)

SAINT-ALBAN:

Ah! You intend to brave the supreme authority

Fair Ninon! Fear that my extreme wrath—

But she will assemble some powerful men

Against whom all my efforts will be insufficient.

Tartuffe will be read; from tonight the great world

Will repeat each verse, each word which scoffs at us.

In town, at Court, we will be jeered

Despite my power, publicly mocked.

Ah! Cursed be Tartuffe, Ninon, and Molière!

And may the whole race of authors be—

But lets seek ways to prevent this evening from—

(Laforet enters.)

LAFORET:

Miz Ninon—I want to see her

Right quick. I'm comin on behalv of her friens.

Tell her that—Mizier? Go tell her t'appear right soon

Tell her dat itz on behalf o her fer frien

D'author, Molière.

SAINT-ALBAN:

Molière! Really—

LAFORET:

You bet.

And I'm known as his servant everywhere.

SAINT-ALBAN:

It's you whom the public for a long time has mentioned

The advice you sometimes give.

LAFORET:

Yes, sir.

I'm the one who every day, for lack of a better opinion

That my dear master consults befoh

Hiz works are received by the public with fine and great approval.

SAINT-ALBAN:

I'm no longer astonished they are so bad.

LAFORET:

Bad! I bet you'd like to have 'em.

SAINT-ALBAN:

Great gods!

LAFORET:

I regret that his last play

Was stopped. Oh! Damn! What pleasure! What intoxication

It w'dda caused t'night. A cursed Saint-Alban

Who acts as if he were the President.

SAINT-ALBAN:

What do you mean?

LAFORET:

This devout Saint-Alban, who knows what t'do

In secret, they say, is messing things up.

So good that our Tartuffe at the moment it's known

Will perhaps be forgotten an' lost forever.

SAINT-ALBAN:

That's a shame!

LAFORET:

It was a play with merit!

In France, there ain't a hypocrite

Who didn' say: Hey, thatz me. They pretend, I think

That Mzier Saint-Alban for the like reasons

Got it expressly forbidden, for fear of bein' recognized—

Between you an' me, let's agree that c'd be the case.

In this play y'see a well-dressed man

Sensual by nature and devote by art

Who contemplates at the same time heaven an' wimmin,

Keepin the body fer hisself and leaving the souls t'God.

But to sell hisself this way, what a dope he is!

P'raps, they w'dnn'a noticed him if he hadna talked

It's often like that, by abusin power

The greatest bring on scorn

And resemble thieves who at the word: rogue

Think somebuddy's a callin them and they say: huh?

SAINT-ALBAN: (furious)

My dear friend—

LAFORET:

Hey, what's up with you?

SAINT-ALBAN:

I beg you, complete

This comparison.

LAFORET: (aside)

He's a Big-Shot, I betcha.

So what, let's continue. (aloud) You are far from knowing

The trick that my master's gonna play this Saint-Alban t'night,

So that the Presidet will lose confidence in him.

He's gotta spread disinformation between them

So that t'mmorra The President will

Angrily reproach Saint-Alban for this clandestine

meetin'

Our way is certain.

SAINT-ALBAN:

Let's see this miracle?

LAFORET:

T'night, when the audience is at our production

It will insist on Tartuffe. Ferbidden works

Are those the public loves bezt.

SAINT-ALBAN:

Go on.

LAFORET:

Molière'll say: Folks, it's impossible.

I'm sensitive to what a nuisance this is to you

But unfortunately, a formal order prevents me

Frum giving you today: Tartuffe or The Impostor.

The President doesn't want it to be performed.

SAINT-ALBAN:

What?

LAFORET:

It's a big breath he'll have in his cheek

The President—

SAINT-ALBAN: (irritated)

That's too much.

LAFORET:

First off, he will ketch it

And then to Saint-Alban he will be right fast to return it

SAINT-ALBAN:

Ah! If Molière dared—

LAFORET:

D'ya get the equivakation?

Let it be played—Oh! I see the publick a laffin at

The poor President, so tricky, so cagey.

I see this Saint-Alban enraged like a dope

He'll urge the Prezident t'avenge this offense.

But on him, from tonight, all the vengeance will fall.

The Prezident'll kick him sayin' in wrath

They're laffin at me; so let 'em laff at you.

SAINT-ALBAN:

May Molière!

LAFORET:

He's gonna do it.

SAINT-ALBAN:

From tomorrow, from tonight—

The laws will do me justice against such a trick

(Molière appears.)

LAFORET:

There's my master.

SAINT-ALBAN:

Molière!

MOLIÈRE:

Ah! Mr. Saint-Alban.

LAFORET: (to Molière)

What, Saint-Alban?

Good God! Save yourself immediately.

MOLIÈRE:

And why?

LAFORET:

I told him everythin'! Oh, What stupidity!

Save yourself.

MOLIÈRE:

Allow me—

SAINT-ALBAN:

I am instructed, Sir,

By your effrontery, and I will teach you

That a magistrate, honest, wise, and revered

Is not made to see himself the object of perfidies

Of a crazy author who writes silly comedies.

MOLIÈRE:

Sir, your outrages cannot affect me;

To respond to them would almost be to deserve them.

The honest magistrate animated by justice

Has the right, I know, to public esteem.

But he soon loses them thanks to his flatterers.

I know in our days of vulgar errors

Each sees his portrait in each comedy

And the author's pride profits by this mania,

If they're grateful that it is a good likeness.

Yes, in the irritated man, I believe I'm seeing that child

Who, shocked by the faults his mirror portrays

Breaks the glass being unable to change them.

SAINT-ALBAN:

Fine, very fine: declaim, Mr. Actor,

Tell us big words which depict nothing.

But as for me, I am going, indeed—to the theatre this very night

When you assemble you idolatrous crows

You will demand the Tartuffe, Look,

There, what will you reply? Will you state your reason?

"The President doesn't want it to be performed."

MOLIÈRE:

Why not?

SAINT-ALBAN:

He admits it brazenly!

Well! My dear sir, you will repent

Of that nasty remark; you will see, you will see

Your play wasn't yet suspended.

From this day you can believe it is forbidden.

(aside) He's calm. (aloud) Moreover, this new masterpiece

Thanks to me, will be burned by the executioner.

(aside) He's not yet upset. (aloud) You'll change your

style,

There are still prisons in this town

(aside) He's smiling. To win the battle let's signal my power.

And know how to prevent his reading tonight.

I will henceforth tell anyone who will listen

That an author is a man—a man to be hanged. (he leaves)

MOLIÈRE:

Well?

LAFORET:

Well?

MOLIÈRE:

How grateful he is!

How he was afraid of it! You saw it, his portrait

Made him go pale with horror

And made him depart, despite himself, from his holy character.

LAFORET:

I indeed paved the way for what just happened.

MOLIÈRE:

How's that?

LAFORET:

I didn't know I must find

Your enemy here; on my soul I thought

That this gentleman was a friend of Madame

And I fearlessly criticized, frankly

The false piety of the cursed Saint-Alban.

MOLIÈRE:

But you criticized him without offering any insults.

LAFORET:

Yes, I only told him the harsh truth

That he was a hypocrite, a—

MOLIÈRE:

But what were you thinking of?

A man who can injure! and what did he reply?

LAFORET:

Why, nothing. he seemed to make a deaf ear.

MOLIÈRE:

Go, he's my precious child the sleeping Lion.

(Ninon appears and listens without entering.)

LAFORET:

My dear master, I fear having done you wrong.

MOLIÈRE:

Why? Haven't I said that even to death

I will attack effrontery, crime and vice?

It's a task, and mission that I must fulfill

I hate and scorn these cowardly censors

Who wish to correct the errors of the century

Giving birth to their books while hiding in the shadows;

As for me, I brave the fools without respecting their numbers

I criticize, censure, and never tremble

Before those whom I offer faithful portraits.

Just as this Saint-Alban by his holy presence

Was unable to contradict me, or constrain me to silence.

He can stop Tartuffe and its author.

But he'll never change my opinions or my heart.

Present or absent though he be, I will repeat endlessly

"Tartuffe is mine, I am proud of my play."

There's not a single feature, a single verse, a single word

That I want to remove from it. An author is really dumb

When he fears some party that blames him

And, trembling, sacrifices a wise epigram

And swallows back in order to please such a lord,

And makes of a brilliant scene a colorless portrait.

I will not imitate this criminal weakness.

I want true success and not caresses.

I need a great reputation, I don't need money;

Public esteem, now there's my treasure.

And I will always know how, without base complacency

To depict what I see, to say what I think—

If my century blames me and fears the truth

At least I will have written for posterity.

NINON: (rushing to Molière)

Molière.

LAFORET:

My dear master!

MOLIÈRE: (aside)

Eh, what, Ninon. (aloud) Madame

You heard me.

NINON:

With heart, mind, and soul—

And I congratulate myself for it: yes, my illustrious friend,

Amongst my finest days, I count this one.

What passion in your speech! what noble energy!

How I recognized the accent of your true genius!

I especially recognized the independent author

Who takes truth for the only bridle for his talent.

Whatever may be your success, you will be too little renowned;

Friend, you think, you speak, like a great man.

MOLIÈRE:

Madame.

LAFORET:

It's the name that one day he will obtain

Everyone agrees he will have earned it.

NINON:

But let's get back, Molière, to the hurried reason

Which made me desire you to visit here.

For you received my letter.

MOLIÈRE:

Yes, Ninon,

And I will keep it.

NINON:

Keep it!

MOLIÈRE:

For truth.

NINON:

That's a word.

MOLIÈRE:

True, but the word is likable,

Your eyes and your mind have a similar power;

A glance depicts love, a word, friendship.

NINON: (smiling)

Most certain is the word—If I've begged you

To come to this place, did you suspect, Molière,

My secret motive?

MOLIÈRE:

No.

NINON:

You are sincere?

MOLIÈRE:

As you are, sometimes.

NINON: (smiling)

I hear you, sir;

Since Tartuffe cannot be performed today

Thanks to this ridiculous and bigoted Saint-Alban

Avenge yourself!

MOLIÈRE:

And how?

NINON:

Without fear or scruple

Come read this work tonight at my place.

MOLIÈRE:

Willingly.

NINON:

My friend, tell me? In good faith

Does this annoy you?

MOLIÈRE:

And why, I beg you?

To read at Ninon's glorifies me.

NINON:

You are very amiable. Then with reason

I am asking some folks of good fashion

Some amateurs and even—I must let you

Guess what friends will hear your play.

MOLIÈRE:

Prince Condé.

NINON:

Oh! Yes, the Prince does justice

To your talents, and imposes himself alone against slanderers.

And then—

MOLIÈRE:

Sevigne, La Chatre.

NINON:

No.

MOLIÈRE:

La Chapelle.

NINON:

Yes, continue.

MOLIÈRE:

Still?

NINON:

The assembly is very fine!

Keep guessing.

MOLIÈRE:

I cannot.

NINON:

Friend, you will see there

The child who was nourished by the Muse Melpomene.

MOLIÈRE:

Corneille!

NINON:

And the other son, less bold, more tender,

Who may one day pretend to the success of Corneille.

MOLIÈRE:

Racine!

NINON:

A cold, malicious, satirical author

But a man full of wit, and the finest taste.

MOLIÈRE:

Boileau! Heaven!—Why—

NINON:

Finally, that author renowned

For his simplicity, candor, and good nature.

Who by a fable teaches the truth

And has painted humanity in a an ant.

LAFORET:

La Fontaine.

MOLIÈRE:

Ninon, before all these models

You want tonight to—

NINON:

Why the Muses must not

Tremble among themselves.

MOLIÈRE:

Those sisters frighten me.

With them quite often wit injures the heart.

And Corneille.

NINON:

Without, you won't love Thalia.

MOLIÈRE:

But the elegant Racine—

NINON:

Loves comedy

In a natural style and yours pleases him.

MOLIÈRE:

Boileau will criticize the plan, the scenes, the subject

He'll say, "All this is bad, the play is detestable,

The characterization false, the intrigue wretched."

NINON:

Boileau judges you worthy of his opinion,

Can he criticize you? You've taken it.

La Fontaine! From him you needn't fear a thing,

Friend of nature, he has to love Molière.

Come on, deliver yourself from a vain terror

And come receive a flattering admiration

Today, interest, friendship, vengeance

Must decide you to this complaisance.

MOLIÈRE:

Friendship suffices for me: of all, this motive

Seems to me the strongest, the nicest.

To obey Ninon, that's seeking to please her,

To please her is to fulfill the earth's desire.

So count on me; I am going to bring you

The manuscript of this writing instantly.

I am less uneasy over the success of the work

For to read before you is already an approval.

LAFORET:

The work is admirable—I trust it will please you.

The two of us have revised it twenty times.

(Molière and Laforet leave.)

NINON: (alone)

Eh! How not to keep Molière for a friend?

My pride enjoys him and my soul is proud of him.

Yes, my tranquility depends on his repose.

Together with him I scorn the envious, the fools.

Together with him I will constantly laugh at their hate.

I will always say to him: "Deliver them to the stage

Deliver us from them despite their confidence and boldness

They will love you even more if they suspect you less.

Don't spare them, they are born to fear you;

You will know how to punish them when you choose to depict them."

Here's Chapelle—Well!

CHAPELLE: (entering)

All your friends will come;

They surrender to such sweet orders

Any moment you will see Racine and Corneille.

NINON:

Prince Condé.

CHAPELLE:

Boileau, La Fontaine.

NINON:

Marvelous,

When Molière reads us a new masterpiece,

Ah! the circle can never be fine enough,

I love true talents of the assembled elite

Because genius is made to judge genius.

CHAPELLE: (delivering a note to her)

Chaulieu alone cannot come to the meeting.

This note—

NINON:

Some beauty must have the march on us.

CHAPELLE:

See—

NINON: (reading)

Beautiful Ninon, an enemy gout

Enchains my crippled limbs,

I see badly, I no longer walk

I'm awake all night, and all day I whine.

But although my sorrow leaves me little hope

The pain of not seeing you

Is my greatest malady;

To be in the midst of my friends

To see Ninon, to hear Molière

Was paradise on earth.

This happiness is no longer permitted me;

I am losing it, pity my disgrace

I curse destiny's laws;

It's too much to suffer these losses at once

Friendship, wit—

CHAPELLE:

And the graces.

NINON:

If he's ill, at least his wit isn't.

CHAPELLE:

What wit is there in singing your charms?

NINON:

I hear someone.

(Enter Corneille, Racine, La Fontaine, Boileau.)

NINON:

It's you, Corneille, La Fontaine, Boileau, Racine, ah, indeed!

CORNEILLE:

To the orders of a Queen.

NINON: (smiling)

Kings often fail.

LA FONTAINE:

Us, Kings?

NINON:

Through talent.

LA FONTAINE:

I have only sheep in my kingdom.

BOILEAU:

And you lead them by the nose.

NINON:

While awaiting Molière,

The Prince Condé who won't be late,

Tell us the Chronicle: have you heard

Some news in Paris today?

RACINE:

Yes,

The honors the great Corneille obtained at court.

NINON:

Is it a pension, income, or the like?

RACINE:

It's a hundred times more.

LA FONTAINE:

What is it then?

NINON:

Explain yourself, speak.

RACINE:

Lords and courtiers were all gathered

To hear The Cid: even with his presence

The monarch was honoring this immense assembly.

After a long hour of waiting and boredom

They are demanding Corneille; he's all that's missing

They demand very loudly: Corneille arrives, passes through

And without greeting him each remains in his seat.

He goes near the king; Louis at his appearance,

Rises, and bows before him with respect.

The Court imitates him, then, although without his diadem

Corneille seems more kingly than the king.

CHAPELLE:

Ah! How fine this scene is! Gentlemen courtiers,

You will learn that it is necessary to honor talent

And you will be less proud.

RACINE:

The anecdote is certain

Because I was a spectator.

NINON:

Tell me, La Fontaine?

The one who ran after you and was laughed at so much.

LA FONTAINE:

Which one?

NINON:

That voyage to Château-Thierry.

CORNEILLE:

Yes, wishing to reestablish peace in his home

He made a long voyage to go see his wife,

Returns without having seen her. Did you fulfill your end?

He told them—Not really, she was in good health.

LA FONTAINE:

I had truly taken care not to disturb my wife

She had so much need of praying for her soul!

NINON:

Racine, your arguments with this dear Boileau

Are they finished?

RACINE:

My wrath is always fresh.

With no discretion, ceaselessly, he criticizes me.

You'd say he prides himself in finding faults.

When I free myself from my work

 Right away, he tells me in an inspired tone

"Twenty times resume your work on the job."

I always have his advice, never his approval.

BOILEAU:

Racine, you think my advice indiscreet.

I criticize you in advance to praise you after.

Effortless glory is really perishable.

You have to earn it if you want it to be durable.

Usurped success has only an instant.

Concentrated efforts can momentarily

Distract the admiration of a nation,

But soon the good taste of time avenges the outrage

Coming to deliver mediocrity to oblivion;

Against posterity intrigue struggles in vain.

The day rises, shines, the shade pales, and is effaced,

The ghost is eclipsed and all receive their place.

A VALET:

The Prince Condé.

ALL:

Milord.

PRINCE CONDÉ:

My friends

It's really nice for me to find myself admitted

In the brilliant circle of graces, of genius.

NINON:

And of valor, Prince, for France is filled

With the report of your exploits.

PRINCE CONDÉ:

Stop talking to me about 'em.

War is a scourge, Gentlemen, to speak of it

Is to offend me, I admit it, a guilty memory.

The more in battle I display a cold, inflexible heart

The more, after I triumph, a secret feeling

Drags me to sorrow and enchains me to remorse.

I distance myself, and return to the breast of our cities

To spend days more pure, less brilliant, more peaceful.

I deliver, at last, calm to my agitated heart

And I rejoice in the arts near beauty.

But now, where is Molière?

NINON: (seeing Laforet)

Ah, there's his serving woman.

What are you doing there?

LAFORET:

Nothing, I was impatient

NINON:

What do you want?

LAFORET: (very low to Ninon)

I was waiting, Madam, for you

To look this way. My master's full of cares.

I think he won't come.

NINON:

Heaven! What have you just told me?

LAFORET: (low)

The President forbids him to read Tartuffe

To you.

NINON:

What! Molière has given in to this order?

LAFORET: (low)

I don't know anything about it, be maebbe so,

It seemz, real dangerous

To laugh at such a plain order.

He hasn't yet consulted me in your biznezz.

PRINCE CONDÉ:

What! Molière could be so cowardly as to be frightened?

CORNEILLE:

May Molière be better appreciated by you!

His soul is incapable of giving in to fear.

RACINE:

He mustn't keep a guilty silence.

NINON:

As for me, I wager, avoiding an unjust suspicion

That he will read Tartuffe.

(Molière appears.)

MOLIÈRE:

And you are right.

Prince—It's fine that an express prohibition

Without cause, without motive, has stopped my play

That they have unjustly despoiled me of my rights!

A hypocrite still intends to choke off my voice!

No.

NINON:

As for me, I was sure from knowing Molière.

LAFORET: (aside)

We've always had a great deal of character.

NINON:

Come on, let's all of us take our places.

LAFORET: (aside)

Now there's truly a scene

Whose painting honors its brush.

(placing herself behind Molière)

As for me, I'll stay here, firstly so as to hear better

Then, if you read badly, I will be able to cue you.

MOLIÈRE:

Tartuffe, a comedy in five acts and in verse.

(Saint-Alban appears.)

SAINT-ALBAN: (aside)

What? He's going to read!

Ah! I'm coming just in time.

MOLIÈRE:

Before beginning, I am going, in a few words,

To expose to your eyes the purpose of this work.

I intend to depict the image of a clever impostor.

LAFORET: (low to Molière)

Saint-Alban is listening to us.

MOLIÈRE: (low)

He's listening to us, good.

(arising, aloud) The hero of my play has the airs and the tone

Of a consummate swindler, of an adroit hypocrite.

Vainly he's feared, fled, avoided.

He has more than one way of being found everywhere.

He always speaks well, and always thinks ill.

He lies from piety, and in conscience deceives us.

And preaches beneficence without ever giving any.

To him, feigning is an art, and injuring is a need.

SAINT-ALBAN: (pointing to himself)

There I am.

NINON:

What?

SAINT-ALBAN: (aside)

Gentlemen, you think me very distant.

NINON:

You are in error: we were, on the contrary, thinking

That we were going to see you.

SAINT-ALBAN: (aside)

That epigram is plain.

PRINCE CONDÉ:

Sit down.

NINON: (low to Prince)

We will all be laughing at him in a moment.

SAINT-ALBAN: (low to the Prince)

Prince, you will hear an impudent work

Which won't appear, which the king forbids.

NINON:

That makes us want to hear it all the more.

SAINT-ALBAN: (low to the Prince)

If by chance this wish seems indiscreet to the king?

PRINCE CONDÉ:

Have you received on this point—?

SAINT-ALBAN:

The order is secret.

PRINCE CONDÉ:

Well, don't talk about it any more.

SAINT-ALBAN:

Without saying more

Of his prohibition, let's speak of the subject of the work.

Here are men of taste, well-known authors

Whose talents and virtues are cited everywhere.

I want to avail myself of their learned admiration

Corneille agrees that such a character.

CORNEILLE:

Is base and vile.

SAINT-ALBAN: (laughing)

Well?

CORNEILLE:

But full of virtue.

SAINT-ALBAN:

What do you mean?

CORNEILLE:

He's the scourge of society

If he didn't degrade Melpomene with his faults

I would have put him on stage before Molière.

SAINT-ALBAN:

He's crazy! You, Boileau, whose reason I admire

Who have, up till now, done nothing but good

Agree that the play is, at least, detestable.

BOILEAU:

Why yesterday La Fontaine told me a certain fable

Which might unite opinion on this point.

Good chap, tell it to us.

LA FONTAINE:

I no longer remember it.

SAINT-ALBAN:

Good.

CHAPELLE:

I know it.

SAINT-ALBAN:

Gentlemen.

PRINCE CONDÉ: (with anger)

Will you be silent?

SAINT-ALBAN:

Prince, be certain of my obedience.

CHAPELLE

The Serpent and the Lime

They tell of a serpent that lived near a clockmaker.

(A bad neighborhood for a clockmaker)

Entered his shop and looked around for something to eat.

Not meeting anything edible

He began to gnaw on a bitter lemon.

This lemon said to him, without making a fuss

Poor ignoramus, hey! What are you trying to do?

You are taking something stronger than you are

Little mad-brained serpent

You can get from me

Only the quarter of a smidgen.

You'll break all your teeth

I only fear time.

That's intended for you, minds of a low order

Who always seek to gnaw on men of talent.

Vainly you torture yourself

Do you think your teeth impress their outrages

On so many fine works?

For you they are brass, steel, diamond.

SAINT-ALBAN:

Bah, bah—

A VALET: (entering)

A page is asking for you, Mr. Molière.

PAGE: (entering)

I'm coming from Lille.

SAINT-ALBAN: (laughing)

Yes, you see they are asking for you.

PAGE:

The order must concern a play.

SAINT-ALBAN:

Ah! I understand

The prohibition—My dear chap, you arrive in time.

ALL:

Read!

NINON:

Whose signature is on this writing?

MOLIÈRE (reading)

Signed. Louis.

(to Ninon) Read, this great name reassures me.

SAINT-ALBAN:

Deign to read it yourself, adorable Ninon.

NINON: (taking the letter)

I am trembling.

MOLIÈRE:

And as for me, I am waiting without emotion.

NINON: (reading)

After having attentively read the comedy of Tartuffe, after having weighed the remarks of our First President who depicts this play as attacking morality, religion and reflecting on personalities, we have found that this masterpiece can offend only hypocrites; therefore we allow, indeed we order, that it be performed in all the cities of France.

MOLIÈRE:

O my King, I owe so much to your extreme justice.

PRINCE CONDÉ:

To honor talent is to honor oneself.

This generous act is worth more than a hundred exploits;

The triumph of the arts makes for the glory of the king.

CORNEILLE:

The Prince, through the effect of this propitious order

Rewards us all by doing you justice.

NINON:

The reading now will be superfluous, I think.

MOLIÈRE:

Laforet, child, run, run to my home quick

So that in all the quarters, the squares, the streets

Ten thousand posters shall be instantly spread

To announce at last to the public of Paris

That Tartuffe will be performed.

NINON:

The public will be very surprised.

SAINT-ALBAN:

What to do now!

A LORD:

Probity leaves you

An excellent way to make the play fail.

LAFORET:

As for me, I'm heading to paradise, if I see some censor

I will shout as loud as I can: Down with the intriguer

And if he shouts louder, as for me I will act in a way

So the public will rise and cry out at him: Out the door.

NINON:

Molière, we all applaud this success.

Your triumph is even our triumph.

But in the breast of happiness, at the fulfillment of glory.

Keep your memory of your friends, of me.

May the spirit, the valor, come into this salon

To find Molière sometimes once more with Ninon.

CURTAIN

SCENE ADDED FOR THE ANNIVERSARY OF MOLIÈRE
by Charles-François-Jean-Baptiste Moreau

This was a scene added to a play called *Le Boulevard Bonne Nouvelle* by Eugène Scribe, Charles-François-Jean-Baptiste Moreau, and M. Mélesville, 1820. It was published separately in 1821 as *Scène Ajoutée au Le Boulevard Bonne Nouvelle*, and was solely the work of Moreau.

CAST OF CHARACTERS

AN ENGLISHMAN

MR. TRICOT

SCENE ADDED FOR THE ANNIVERSARY OF MOLIÈRE

ENGLISHMAN:

Oh! Sir—is the Théâtre Français around here?

TRICOT:

Oh! No, Sir, we are quite a ways from it.

ENGLISHMAN:

So much the better; I'm very happy.

TRICOT:

Why's that, sir?

ENGLISHMAN:

Why? That Devil of a Molière bores me a lot, and every day on all the—all the—what do you call these papers attached to walls?

TRICOT:

Ah! Posters.

ENGLISHMAN:

Yes, I meant to say that I see his name on all the posters in huge letters.

TRICOT:

That's not surprising. (singing)

It's right they celebrate the happy day,

Marking the birth of Molière.

For his good deeds, it's a just return

Don't criticize our gratitude.

By illustrating in all his works

With all the art, the nation is his mother.

France in its happiest days

Has created a thousand heroes

But has only seen one Molière born.

ENGLISHMAN:

GODDAM! That's one too many.

TRICOT:

May one know where this prejudice you have against him proceeds from?

ENGLISHMAN:

Oh! I just can't stand him.

TRICOT:

But what's the reason?

ENGLISHMAN:

The reason is I can't stand him.

TRICOT:

Perhaps the gentleman doesn't know him?

ENGLISHMAN: (laughing)

Ouf! I know him perfectly well, I swear to you; I've had him played very often in my country house where Milady puts on very magnificent and expensive performances.

TRICOT:

It was you who paid?

ENGLISHMAN:

Yes. They put on comedies at my expense: I recall that it was a Member of Parliament who played Tartuffe, and Milady, my wife, had a part in "Georges, beaten and satisfied."

TRICOT:

Ah! Georges Dandin.

ENGLISHMAN:

Yes. It was I who played Dandin. The play was very much in fashion, and they laughed a lot at me.

TRICOT:

Since you owe such a success to Molière, I can't conceive why you cannot stand him.

ENGLISHMAN:

Because of personal considerations: for I am, like all Englishmen, a great admirer of Molière. That devil of a man ruined me.

TRICOT:

Not possible!

ENGLISHMAN:

It's very possible. I had an uncle, totally rich and very miserly; very agreeable expectation for his heirs! Well, because he saw Harpagon, he became a bit dissipated; and he didn't allow himself to lack anything; he drank, he ate every day, that's quite a terrible thing for me.

TRICOT:

Now I understand your rage against Molière.

ENGLISHMAN:

That was nothing yet. I had a very old uncle, who had 20,000 pounds sterling in income, and he was attacked by the spleen—at least that's what the family hoped.

(singing) Sad and pained, as its shadow enveloped him

He meditated a funereal plan.

When, by chance, he saw The Misanthrope

Suddenly he hesitated.

Pourceaugnac with the apothecary

Had almost made him sprightly,

And The Imaginary Invalid cured him completely.

(speaking) All he did was laugh. He kept talking about Thos Diafoirus, and when I asked him for money, he told me: Clisterium donare, ensuita purgare. That was something to hang oneself for.

TRICOT:

No question, it's a horror—An author who cures the spleen in your own home, that's unheard of.

ENGLISHMAN:

Indeed, I thought so. We have Lord Byron who would be capable of giving it by himself to all England; but that's not all, yet—I had an aunt.

TRICOT:

Ah, my God, what a family.

ENGLISHMAN:

Who wrote long novels, as long as Lady Morgan, which sold as highly priced as Walter Scott. She has the misfortune of seeing at Argitti-Rooms The Learned Ladies.

TRICOT:

Ah! The Learned Ladies.

ENGLISHMAN:

Yes. And she threw into the fire, the first ten volumes of a little novel for which the London Library was offering 6,000 guineas—and I needed to pay my debts with my aunt's novel.

TRICOT:

I conceive that between Molière and you, it's war to the death.

ENGLISHMAN:

And I got here just in time for the Anniversary, for you are quite sure this was the anniversary?

TRICOT:

Sir, they say so. It's one of my habits. The bell-ringer of Saint Eustache who made this discovery in the registry of the Parish.

ENGLISH:

It would appear, then, that the place of his birth?

TRICOT:

Sir, it's not known.

ENGLISHMAN:

Ah! And the exact day?

TRICOT:

That's not certain.

ENGLISHMAN:

But—his tomb?

TRICOT:

Sir, that's very uncertain.

ENGLISHMAN: (singing)

You must agree, you are economical

In the honors you owe the gifted.

If we have less great men than you

We burn more incense on their altars.

Do justice to England

Your Molière, applauded so many times

Hardly obtains a little plot of ground;

Garrick reposes beside our kings.

TRICOT: (singing)

It's too true; through a blind rage

This great man was outraged.

But the prejudices of a former age

Have been avenged by our century.

The obscure man has entirely succumbed

But Molière is still standing.

Who cares where his tomb may be

His genius is everywhere.

(speaking) And, Sir, I must not hide from you, that the modest Gymnasium Theatre is also allowing itself to celebrate the anniversary of his birth today.

ENGLISHMAN:

Goddam!—This Molière who persecuted me, who had pursued all the ridiculous—

TRICOT:

You cannot escape him.

(The scene changes and represents the interior of a temple at the back of which can be seen a bust of Molière placed on a pedestal. All the actors of the Prologue are grouped around him, and are preparing to crown him.)

GENERAL CHORUS:

Let's celebrate the prosperous day

When the first of authors

First saw the light.

And on the face of Molière

Let's place some modest flowers.

AGNES: (singing)

O Molière! O astonishing and sublime genius!

You that we admire without daring to flatter

May you deign to count us among your children.

Pardon our audacity because of the flame that animates us,

May our love legitimize us;

And let's be your children, at least to celebrate you.

(she approaches the bust of Molière and places a crown of laurels on his head)

TRICOT: (singing)

Shakespeare may appear gay

To the lords of England.

Schiller is very intriguing

His touch is light

But his drama fatiguing.

With his controlled verve,

I like Molière better, hey-ho

I like Molière better.

MR. DUJOUR: (singing)

The art of joining to entertainment

Strict reason;

The art of gaily pursuing

Haughty stupidity;

The art of depicting, one after another—

The man of heart, the bourgeois

Weren't those hearts born

The day of Molière's birth?

GEORGETTE: (singing)

This great man whose writings

Charmed the whole of France

Weren't scorned by the opinion

Of his cook

You know how he listened to her.

And since he consulted her

You can be proud when you are

Molière's servant.

INVALID: (singing)

The doctors that he mocked,

That so proud faculty,

Tartuffe's that he revealed

Their souls in entirety;

You even fear his name

When you see the house

Where Molière was born

ENGLISHMAN: (singing)

How many scenes do we see

In our England

Of elections

and of Ministers

Of budgets with stipends

As comic as slapstick?

That's what one doesn't find

At home with Mr. Molière.

MADAME CHINCHILLA: (singing to the Audience)

Sometimes for our songs

A severe audience

Mixes its uproar with our noisy lyrics

Certain rumors of war

Too often take their turn

Let them be silent at least

For the anniversary of the day

That Molière was born.

All repeat the general chorus:

Let's celebrate the prosperous day

When the first of authors

First saw the light.

And on the face of Molière

Let's place some modest flowers.

CURTAIN

THE KING IS WAITING
by George Sand

CAST OF CHARACTERS

MOLIÈRE

SHADES

SOPHOCLES

AESCHYLUS

EURIPIDES

SHAKESPEARE

VOLTAIRE

BEAUMARCHAIS

LA GRANGE

DUCROISY

BRÉCOURT

BÉJART

FIRST ORDERLY

SECOND ORDERLY

THIRD ORDERLY

FOURTH ORDERLY

FIFTH ORDERLY

THE MUSE

LAFORET

MADAME MOLIÈRE

MISS DUPARC

MISS DUCROISY

MISS BÉJART

MISS HERVÉ

MISS DE BRIE

THE KING IS WAITING

LAFORET:

Come on, Mr. Molière, my master, if you please, sit down to eat and don't forget that your play is not finished.

MOLIÈRE:

Fine! Fine! It will be in a minute; I have only one scene to write.

LAFORET:

But your actors and especially your actresses, pretend not to know their business.

MOLIÈRE: (seated and working)

I am awaiting them here for rehearsal, and I intend to write the ending while they are rehearsing the opening scenes.

LAFORET:

Ah! Sir, you cannot think of it! Are you insisting that they study, that they rehearse, that they play, almost at the same time? For His Majesty the King will be here in two hours and is counting on you to be ready.

MOLIÈRE:

The king will be indulgent.

LAFORET:

Kings have none for what concerns their amusement. Truly, my master, you've taken on a responsibility really heavy to want to make folks laugh who only laugh if they choose to. The king doesn't want to know that you are sick and that your poor body suffers for all the ills you give yourself. You hardly leave your bed, and it must be that you are already writing a prologue for a play that you have caused to be studied and rehearsed, and that you are taking your role yourself, (aside) He's not listening to me. So much the better! for to babble this way I can only delay him. My poor master! he's all changed color and very thin lately.!

MOLIÈRE: (throwing a sheet on his manuscript)

Here, read it carefully, and if something shocks you, tell me in a few words.

LAFORET: (taking the pen)

That's it, I will mark the places that I do not understand.

MOLIÈRE: (interrupting her)

Lucky intelligence of those who have learned nothing, and who find in themselves these manners of speech which flourish in our language and once arranged are incomparable. Ah! Laforet, it's you who are the author of my best scenes!

LAFORET:

Not at all, master! It still must pass through your scrawl to signify something, and the truth is that the two of us have a great deal of wit.

MOLIÈRE: (smiling and writing)

You think so?

LAFORET:

Oh! first off, we speak in a manner that everybody understands and doesn't burn the ears of Christians. All those who go to hear your plays and return charmed. in some degree they will be, and as the king says, how you make the stones laugh, folks like me say it, too, and laugh without asking permission. My opinion is, sir, that we speak much better than those snobs of the court who you have so aptly portrayed, that they believe they are listening to themselves speak.

MOLIÈRE: (tossing away his pen)

I'm finished. What time is it?

LAFORET:

You've still got an hour; but your actors haven't arrived. Ah! Sir, here we are like the day of The Impromptu of Versauilles, in which no one knew his part, and where you were so much in pain, that you became sick over it,. What wouldn't I give to see you away from all this! A little disgrace by the king wouldn't injure your health, believe me.

MOLIÈRE:

The Impromptu was nonetheless very well played and my comrades surpassed themselves. A little haste and a feverish night don't injure the success of things. But see here our folks are coming. Let's not lose any time.

(Enter Brécourt, La Grange, Ducroisy, Miss Duparc, Miss Béjart, Miss De Brie, Madame Molière, Miss Ducroisy, and Miss Hervé)

MOLIÈRE:

Come along, ladies and gentlemen! are you mocking yourself with your torpor? Here's the end of our play.

DUCROISY:

Ah! By my word, Molière, it's you who are making fun of us to think that we can possibly learn and play at the same moment. For my part, I swear to you indeed, that I renounce it. (casting his part angrily on the table)

BRÉCOURT:

Sonofabitch! gentlemen, what do you want to screw up today for?

DUCROISY:

What do you want us to do? We don't know our parts, and it's just to enrage us to force us to perform this way.

MOLIÈRE:

Ah! strange animals have led these actors!

LA GRANGE:

The technique of performing when one doesn't know the part?

MISS DUPARC:

As for me, I declare to you that I cannot remember a word of my character.

MISS DE BRIE:

I really know that it will be necessary to shift mine from one end to the next.

MISS BÉJART:

And as for me, I am quite prepared to hold my script in my hand.

MADAME MOLIÈRE:

And me, too.

MISS HERVÉ:

As for me, I have no great thing to say.

MISS DUCROISY:

Me neither, but with this, I won't be responsible for failing.

MISS DE BRIE: (to Molière)

So much the worse for you! You ought to have taken better precautions and not undertaken what you've have done in a week.

MOLIÈRE:

The way to protect myself when the king has ordered

it?

MADAME MOLIÈRE:

That's all well and good, husband of mine; but if the king demands the impossible—

MOLIÈRE:

Wife, shut up, are you an animal?

MADAME MOLIÈRE:

Thanks a lot! See how marriage changes folks entirely; you wouldn't have said that eighteen months ago.

MOLIÈRE:

I beg you, shut up.

MADAME MOLIÈRE:

As for me, I care no more about it, and there's no king here who clings to it. I do not know a word of the play, and if the king is not satisfied let him take it our on you.

MOLIÈRE:

My wife, let's all calm down, if you please. The king is not far off and might hear you!

MADAME MOLIÈRE:

I won't let it go. If I have no memory, the king cannot make me have one, and I find that it is not the bother of you making fun of courtiers, for them to come say what they are saying and do what they are doing.

MOLIÈRE:

Oh! plague be on women and their tongues! Let's think of rehearsing if you please.

LA GRANGE:

If you please, let's give it up. It's really an impossible thing to do what we are asked to do. to put it on stage and to recite things that one doesn't know. I am your valet but a thousand crowns won't get me to play.

DUCROISY:

Nor I, for twenty-five blows with a whip.

MOLIÈRE:

My God, I hear an uproar; assuredly it is the king arriving, and I see plainly that we won't have time to go any further. Now that's what it is to quarrel. Well, for the rest, do the best you possibly can.

MISS BÉJART:

On my word, terror is seizing me, and I won't know how to perform my part, if I don't rehearse it completely.

MOLIÈRE:

What, you won't know how to perform you part?

MISS BÉJART:

No.

MISS DUPARC:

Mine neither.

MISS DE BRIE:

Mine neither.

MADAME MOLIÈRE:

Nor I.

MISS HERVÉ:

Nor I.

MISS DUCROISSY:

Nor I.

MOLIÈRE:

So what are you thinking of doing? Are you all making fun of me?

(Béjart enters.)

BÉJART:

Gentlemen, I am coming to inform you that the king has come and that he is waiting for you to begin.

MOLIÈRE:

Ah! sir, you see me in the greatest difficulty in the world. Here are terrified women who say they must rehearse their parts before beginning. We ask mercy for yet another moment. (to actresses) Hey! for God's sake try to get hold of yourselves. Be courageous, I beg you.

MISS DUPARC:

You ought to excuse yourself.

MOLIÈRE:

What do you mean, excuse myself?

(Enter an Orderly)

FIRST ORDERLY:

Gentlemen, will you begin!

MOLIÈRE:

Right away, sir,. I think that I am losing the spirit of this business, and—

(Second orderly enters)

SECOND ORDERLY:

Gentleman, will you begin!

MOLIÈRE:

In a moment, sir! (to his comrades) Hey, come on; would you want me to affront him—?

THIRD ORDERLY: (entering)

Gentlemen, will you begin?

MOLIÈRE:

Yes, sir, we are going there! Hey, what people are starting the party and are coming to say: Will you start, unless the king has not ordered them to.

FOURTH ORDERLY:

Gentlemen, get started!

MOLIÈRE:

That's what is happening, sir. (to his comrades) What then! Will I be confounded?

FIFTH ORDERLY:

Gentlemen, the king risks being kept waiting.

SIXTH ORDERLY:

Gentlemen, the king is waiting.

SEVENTH ORDERLY:

Gentlemen, the king has waited.

MISS DE BRIE:

As for us, it only remains for us to take a role and to save ourselves.

MISS DUPARC:

It's what is suitable to do. Molière can get out of it as best he can.

MISS HERVÉ:

I think like you.

MISS DUCROISY:

That's my opinion, and save yourself if you can.

MADAME MOLIÈRE: (to her husband)

So, this is well done, and see the result of your bull-headedness.

(All the actors and orderlies leave. Molière remains alone and confounded.)

MOLIÈRE:

The king is waiting, the king has been kept waiting! I am a desperate man, a ruined man, a dead man! Ah! Cursed be the hour that I accepted the commands of a king, the renown of an author, and the livery of an actor! Cursed be my wife! cursed be my troupe! cursed be my play!! (he strides about in agitation) Oh the strange weakness, and terrible blindness of risking thus the interests of his honor, for the ridiculous thought of a chimeric duty! Is it not vanity which advised me to make a comedy in so short a time? And my wife wasn't she right to reproach me for having played the courtier by acting in such a way? (he strides about) Assuredly, when I consider my life, it seems to me only that I've been surrounded by reproach and hypocrisy, this fashionable vice which enjoys, in repose, a sovereign impunity. At all times, I've advised myself that the character of a man of wealth is the best that can be played, and if I noticed the attachment of the king, it's that his kindness made me obligated to him, more than his power made me his servant. Yes, my heart, I think that you are honest, and that you are more sensitive to marks of esteem than to the favors of fortune. Without that, wherein would lie the truth of my attachment? What's a king? A man of power to do good, and it's only when he does it that he distinguishes himself from other men. From what proceeds the great mortification of displeasing a king, when one is so little restrained from displeasing men of wealth who are not to be feared? Your head was really wise, Molière, the day that it found itself not well protected in your father's shop? Why didn't you remain a simple artisan as birth had destined you to be, rather than run through the world after glory and fortune? It's that the function of comedy is to correct vices through pleasant lessons, and that nothing better reforms most people than depicting their faults; it's because heaven has given you this sight which pierces the veil of lies, and this art of putting light on them, through clever poems, that the bad and the stupid bear in the depths of themselves. and could they accuse me of scorning the condition from which I emerged because I vividly censure the rogueries and ugliness of those who think themselves above all condition? No, Molière, you haven't failed, and if the king uses you to chastise his court, you use yourself to avenge all those court folks who want to disparage you.

Come on, I feel these reflections have put my mind in better mood, and that I can wait, without much shame and weakness, the prince's displeasure. He's a man that knows our genius has its weariness just like his power, and my wife was not mistaken in saying that it doesn't depend on a monarch to give us appropriate memory or talent. (he sits down) Will he restore my health that I have lost in a thousand labors for the honor of letters, for the advantage of my comrades? No, these kings that equal themselves to the gods cannot control nature. Nature alone can, by itself, when we let it do so, extract itself easily from the disorder into which it has fallen.

I feel a great weariness—but my mind, satisfied, is lost in contemplation of the eternal world in which my life is only a small drop in a vast ocean. Other poets have preceded me, they suffered as well, and the masters that I studied every day, found strength in the sentiment of goodness they inspired in mankind. Others will come who will study me and interpret me in their turn in a new tongue. May they be less ill in body and as sane in mind as I feel myself at this hour.

(He dozes off. A cloud slowly envelops him; a musical chorus sings behind the cloud. When the cloud dissipates, the shades of ancient poets are to be seen standing around Molière. Terence, Aeschylus, Plautus,

Sophocles, Euripides, Shakespeare, Voltaire, Rousseau, Marivaux, Sedaine, Beaumarchais, etc. The Muse of Drama is in the midst of them, quite close to Molière.)

MUSE:

Sleep, o cherished poet! May your generous and pure soul taste the blessings of rest, while awaiting the day on which, on this stage, illustrious through your works, you will sleep for a last time so as to awake in the breast of the gods. O Molière, you are not deceived, and the thoughts in the midst of which the vision surprises you are like distant voices of your forerunners who join with those of your posterity to tell you " Courage, o friend of truth, censor of vice! you are ill, you languish, but you are singing, you are working; son of an artisan, light of a nation, always taking advice from a child of the people. Have confidence, friend! if the cares of the world consume you, if the greats of the world disdain you, if the hypocrites persecute you, your avenger awakes: human reason, the logic of the nation will preserve you from forgetfulness, and in the future, you will be no longer the amusement of a court, but the blazon of a nation. Here they are around you, your immortal brothers, these poets of the past and the future who now invoke your thoughts. Show yourself to him in his dream, illustrious masters, and support with your words his defeated soul. Tell him he's not cradled by a vain illusion by believing human dignity. Tell him that truth is for all times, and that it grows in the night of the ages, like the light of a torch. The first ones come: fathers of ancient tragedy, primitive poets! Aeschylus, Sophocles, Euripides! and may the eternal oracle of wisdom echo in the heart of new men.

AECHYLUS:

They say the gods don't deign to concern themselves with men who crowd at the feet of glory's most holy laws. To speak this way is to be impious. More than once they have seen the descendants who breathe the air of injustice, intoxicated by a funereal opulence. Possess only blessings without peril. Necessity is wisdom. Wealth is a weak rampart for a man who insolently kicks over the altars of justice.

Justice preserves its dazzle, even in smoky hovels. But gold and fortune do not blind it when the hands are soiled. It flees, it seeks a more holy dwelling!

May discord, insatiable crimes never allow themselves to sound their tremors in the city of free men, Never let the blood of citizens irrigate the dust and never, murder set itself up in Athens to revenge murder! May the interest of the State carry with it into the heart, and may the citizens be full of mutual love. Unity is the remedy of all mortal ills.

SOPHOCLES:

May I only be transported into the place where the arms of valiant fighters make echo the clash of arms of deliverance! I envy the luck of all who may be witness to their glory. O you, who perish in defense of your domestic altars, your tomb will always be a more formidable rampart against the enemy than a thousand fighters.

The holy laws of truth are not always sufficient to sustain mankind against the outrages of men. But, sooner or later, the gods punish the unworthy profaners of sacred things. Know, impious worshippers of slavery, that you are reduced to the fate that you made mankind submit to. By depriving them of liberty, you will lose yours. The orders of an impious mortal are not strong enough to prevail over unwritten laws, immutable works of the gods. They are not of today or yesterday. No one knows their origin, but they are always living.

THE MUSE:

Unwritten laws of the human conscience, you will be written now by the hand of men, and sworn to on the altars of the fatherland. In your turn, suave Euripides, tell us the truth of your soul, superior to that of your age.

EURIPEDES:

Written laws are given to the weak and are powerful rights of equality. The least of citizens dares to reply proudly to the arrogant rich man who insults him, and the smallest, if the law is with him, will succeed over the most grand.

Equality directly unites friends to friends, city to city, nation to nation. Between the greatest and the smallest there has been an eternal war, but mortals don't possess their own riches; they belong to the gods, and we are their depositaries. When they want them, they retake them.

I've seen indulgence in the soul of the rich, and generosity in the soul of the poor.

The breast of a mortal often encloses the laws of the future, and the Muse sings the promises of Jupiter the Liberator. O earth, you know the path of justice: do not allow anyone to ravish from you the glory of obeying the gods. Minerva has given a taste of the delicious liqueur of hope to the poor as well as the opulent.

MUSE:

Shakespeare, great tragedian and philosopher of the renaissance of letters, speak to the dreaming poet, too. Voltaire, precursor of a great revolution; Beaumarchais powerful force of a memorable struggle, tell by whom and how his work will be continued.

SHAKESPEARE:

These new times are filled with strange events. The whole massive earth has shivered like an unsafe machine, and tempests and storms have risen in which furious winds have shattered the trunks of old oak trees. The slave has raised his left hand in the air, it has a torch like twenty conjoined torches, and his hand, insensitive to the flame, remains without being scalded. Cassius will free Cassius from slavery. There it is, great gods! that you have placed an invincible force on the weak! That's the way you thwart tyrants. Neither the stone tower nor bronze walls worked, nor the airless dungeon, nor massive irons can enchain the strength of the soul. (to Sophocles, Aeschylus and Euripides) Oracles of antiquity, I, too, have prophesized; that's the mission of poets, that's the inheritance that the dead leave to the living. As for me, I was not one of those who supported injustice with a serene face, and if sometimes I laughed like Molière, like Molière I had a serious soul and face.

VOLTAIRE: (holding Jean-Jacques Rousseau by the hand)

I was quick in my time to the place of the living and the dead. But the dead are calm and much less jealous than the others. I did enough so I can sleep peacefully after a long battle; I reduced the past to ashes; I crushed infamous intolerance; I made a great revolution. Rousseau made a second. The two of us edified the future, and France protected our two crowns which touched without mutually withering in the hand of Liberty.

BEAUMARCHAIS:

Great Molière, I admire the serenity of your sleep and the equality of your soul! Mine was an alembic and my life a storm. You bequeathed me Sgnarelle and Scapin from whom I made Figaro; and Figaro has stirred up the town and gown, the kings and the people. He hastened the fall of those who had had only the trouble of being born; he rehabilitated intelligence; he withered with bitterness the shackles that the stupidity and immorality of favorites of fortune wanted to rivet to the ties of nature. I unmasked the prevaricating judge; I railed almost to blood the wit of censure. I said, and I repeat, that stupidities imprinted have no more importance than chains in which one inhibits the stream, and that without the liberty of blaming, it is no flattering praise. I've said that only small men suspect small writings. All that I have said pierced like a skewer, if not engraved like an engraving tool . Son of an artisan like you, Molière, I avenged the artisan for the scorn of the great. Now, my task is finished. Nature vindicated me, Providence avenged me.

MUSE:

The time for vengeance is passed! Human reason has triumphed, the obstacle is destroyed, the path is open, arise, poets of the future! How beautiful; it is, poetry which is preparing itself,! which is great! art which is going to be born from the breath of liberty! O you who come to pick the flowers on this fruitful earth, don't forget that it was for a long while irrigated with blood, sweat, and tears. Think that your fathers found it uncultivated and that they inseminated life into it. Remember that they have no glory of talent except grandeur of thought, and that genius is sterile if the heart is cold. Warm your self by this eternal fireside whose true poets have made the spark flourish. Stroll in, flame over the world, and let the radiance of free France be heard from dawn to dusk.

Awake, Molière, and you, immortal shades, climb back to your heaven, that sanctuary where the human soul reinvigorates itself, and from which the blessings of the genius of the dead, fall back, ceaselessly on the living like fecund rain.

(The cloud ascends, is lost during a chorus of music, and the vision disappears.)

LAFORET:

Hey! For the love of God, master, what are you doing here when the whole world is asking for you and the king is calling for you.

MOLIÈRE:

You say that the king is calling for me? Are there still kings? I am awaking from a true chaos in which it seemed to me everything had changed name, fashion and language on earth. It was making a noble and strong enough honest company all together. Would you also be in a lethargy, my poor Laforet?

LAFORET:

Lethargy as much as you wish, sir, but the king is in the hall, the king fills the hall completely from top to bottom.

MOLIÈRE:

Ah! My word, I am mad, or it's you who've lost judgment, my servant. Who is it that will judge me now, if Laforet becomes unreasonable?

LAFORET:

But, sir, turn about a little, and rather look around. You will see if I am lying. Look there where the king who has waited for you for the last hour and try to excuse yourself by turning some handsome compliment in your manner.

MOLIÈRE: (approaching the ramp and looking into the hall, placing his hand before his eyes.)

The king? I don't see the king; where could he be hiding?

LAFORET: (behind him)

Still make your excuse; you will see him later.

MOLIÈRE: (bowing)

Sire!

(He stops, crossing his arms and remains pensive.)

LAFORET:

Hey, for mercy sakes, or the devil take me if you are not hissed.

MOLIÈRE: (absorbed)

Let me alone, Laforet, don't wake me, I'm still dreaming, but as I dream, my mind is releasing itself from its burdens and I feel my courage inflate. I indeed see a king, but he's no longer called Louis XIV; he's called The People! The sovereign people! It's a word that I didn't know, a great word like eternity! This sovereign here is great too, greater than all the kings, because he is good, because he has no interest in deceiving, because instead of courtiers he has brothers. Ah! Yes, I recognize him now, for I am he, also, me, of that powerful race, in which genius and the heart go hand in hand, What! not a single marquis, not a pedantic lady, not a fat financier, not a Tartuffe, not a bore, not a Porceaugnac? I tell you not to awaken me, Laforet, for I am, this time, in a good dream, which is explaining so much to me.

LAFORET:

By Jove, sir, where will you get your marquis now? Those were fine days when you did justice, so that all the villainous folks that you have sketched in a good manner, so well portrayed that they no longer show their faces anywhere.

MOLIÈRE: (turning towards his servant)

And the doctors? Are there still doctors?

LAFORET:

Yes, sir, there are still some, but they kill far fewer folks than in oure\ days. Come, enough babbling, pay the new sovereign your compliment.

MOLIÈRE:

I'm afraid he won't laugh because of the old language we are using.

LAFORET:

Hey! Say it any way. All men are alike in words, and it is only in actions that they discover themselves to be different. You see that I know you by heart.

MOLIÈRE: (very moved)

Gentlemen—

LAFORET: (in a low voice)

You must say citizens, these days.

MOLIÈRE:

Are we then in Rome or in Sparta? Praise God! I really wish it. But no, I feel that we are better still in Paris. Citizens, The Theatre of The Republic is happy to open its doors to you all wide, and it invites you to enter it often. It's the great Corneille, it's the sweet Racine, interpreters of the great tragedies of antiquity; it's the astonishing Shakespeare, it's the naive Sedaine, it's the brilliant Beaumarchais, it's the tender Marivaux, it's the potent Voltaire, it's all the ancients and all the moderns, in the end, it's old Molière who will do you the honors. We won't provide you those pompous prologues that were addressed to kings. One doesn't flatter those one esteems. We have good things to serve you, and we know they will be agreeable to you, having offered the best that we can.

CURTAIN

CYRANO AND MOLIÈRE
by George Jubin

To Carmen,
who would make a great Madeleine

TRANSLATOR'S NOTE

Just as the English occasionally like to write plays about Shakespeare, the French are fond of writing plays about Molière. Indeed, it's been a cottage industry over the years, especially in the nineteenth century. Unlike their English counterparts, the French do a better job of it, because they do not allow their admiration for Molière to degenerate into hagiography. Both Molière and Cyrano de Bergerac studied under the philosopher Gassendi. I do not know what, if any, personal relationship the great soldier swordsman and the comic writer had. That Molière, was originally Poquelin, a son of the King's upholsterer, is undoubtedly true. That he followed Madeleine Béjart onto the stage, abandoning the law his father destined him for, is historical. The rest is unknown, but cleverly put together by the author George Jubin. About the author or the circumstances under which the play was performed, I know nothing. I came across the book one day in the stacks in the McKeldin Library at the University of Maryland. I thought the title was interesting, but didn't have time to read it. When later I decided to look at it again, the book was gone. Several years went by. I couldn't find it. One day I looked it up in the catalogue and found it had been moved to the Rare Book Department.

—Frank J. Morlock

CAST OF CHARACTERS

JEAN-BAPTISTE POQUELIN

CYRANO DE BERGERAC

MADELEINE BÉJART

CYRANO AND MOLIÈRE

December 1643. At the Jeu de Paume des Metayers, cradle of the Illustre Théâtre on the eve of its opening.

The stage represents a room adjoining the Jeu de Paume (Tennis Court) on the first floor that serves as a lodging for Madeleine Béjart and Jean-Baptiste Poquelin. In the back a large judas-door giving on the stairway to the street. To the left, a large window giving on the Tennis Court (Jeu de Paume.) To the right, mid-stage, a chimney and on each side of it two small doors leading to the Tennis Court. A trunk and a table.

Poquelin is walking about in agitation. As the door opens he throws the papers in the trunk and turns ill-humoredly towards Madeleine as she enters.

POQUELIN:

Where are you coming from?

MADELEINE: (ridding herself of her cloak)

What's that to you?

POQUELIN:

Eh! I mean to know!

MADELEINE: (heading towards the door to the Tennis Court)

That gallant tone again. Oh, in that case, goodbye!

POQUELIN:

Madeleine! (she turns toward him) This game has to end! Because your way of behaving is putting me through torture. Heavens, yesterday again—that rustic with an impertinent manner; that financier came to our rehearsal. You received him like a balm, an exquisite balm. His compliments worthy of a fool.

MADELEINE:

Well, I've received them from Poquelin and others even better fashioned.

POQUELIN:

Here?

MADELEINE:

No, in the street! From a gallant cavalier who, as soon as he'd seen me, said a thousand sweet nothings to me from the Pont Neuf almost to our lodging.

POQUELIN:

You didn/t have the cheek, I think, to reply.

MADELEINE: (evasively)

Hmmm!

POQUELIN:

I feel rage gripping me. To please everyone and to try to be displeasing to me alone! Me, who loves you. (more softly) And who's proved it to you!

MADELEINE: (interrupting him)

Proved it? There we go. The word's come. Proved it? By your somber and melancholy humor and by your words crabbed with jealous tyranny? Yes, I know. For me you became an actor. The job of an upholsterer no longer called you. Caprice on your part.

POQUELIN: (excitedly)

But you were something else than a caprice on my part! You were one of those that one hardly dares contemplate at a distance, that suddenly a happy chance puts in your path, in your life, and then one loves without being loved in return and one is jealous, jealous to the point of rage! You lack a heart to give unconditionally. You've only given me a shadow of love!

MADELEINE: (coquettish)

Poquelin, my friend, you are difficult! And I know more than one in this fine town who would be content with that ghost.

POQUELIN: (abruptly)

Well, as for me, I demand something more!

MADELEINE: (ironic)

Behold! My sweet, the misfortune is I am incapable of offering you anything better! (pause) After all, am I so much at fault? I'm a coquette? Eh, yes! Isn't that our job, the rest of us? To bring men under our rule and to see them all on their knees begging for a smile, and make them delirious for a sweet look? Why that's our job. The profession demands it. We must please. (laughing) And why deny it, we please willingly.

POQUELIN:

That's what I deplore. (changing tone) Besides, what's the use of quarreling again? You can go spend your time with all your stupid gallants. As for me, I cannot suffer their insolent remarks. Henceforth they will never come to my ears!

MADELEINE: (uneasy)

What are you saying?

POQUELIN: (determined)

I am going to leave.

MADELEINE: (excitedly)

What? On the eve of the day we are opening this theatre?

POQUELIN:

Forthwith! Right now.

MADELEINE:

And your part then?

POQUELIN:

Someone will learn to replace me soon.

MADELEINE:

In an hour?

(aside) He's crazy!

(to Poquelin) Why, Poquelin, look—you know perfectly well that no one can replace you this way.

POQUELIN:

So much the worse for you!

MADELEINE: (persuasively)

And for you, too! Because, in the end, aren't you interested in how our Illustre Théâtre—?

POQUELIN:

Bah! It will be illustrious without me.

MADELEINE: (desolated)

Stubborn! (she sits down in apparent consternation)

POQUELIN: (observing her, bitterly)

Ah! How upset you get when it's your interest that's threatened.

MADELEINE: (raising her head)

Mercy!

POQUELIN:

And, when you see me ready to leave—!

MADELEINE: (rising, conciliatory)

Well then, if it angers you so much, I will control this coquetry.

POQUELIN:

Get out!

MADELEINE:

Honestly.

POQUELIN: (hesitating)

Really true?

MADELEINE:

No admirer will come here anymore.

POQUELIN:

And your admirer of just now—in the street?

MADELEINE: (lying)

An invented story! (coaxingly) Come on, don't put on your sad face any more—big jealous. (she is near the window and watches the Tennis Court) And wait—Go on, they're waiting for you to rehearse.

POQUELIN:

Is the author there?

MADELEINE:

Mr. Tristan? Yes, certainly. (she half opens the window and speaking to the wings) He's coming to join you! (to Poquelin who goes toward the door) By the way, your tirade when Crispin says he's dying of fire! Some bravado. (smiling) I'm a good adviser for the profession.

POQUELIN:

Thanks! (starts to leave and turns toward Madeleine) But if some gallant were to appear here—.

MADELEINE: (pushing him out)

You will leave. Yes. But get going will you?

POQUELIN:

You're coming down?

MADELEINE:

No, my scene isn't until the end of the act. (Poquelin leaves) Whew! How much trouble it takes to put this damned Poquelin straight! (thoughtful) Jealous! (laughing) It falls out well. My heart is a mill that turns with every puff of wind. (seriously) The important thing is for him to stay. To leave us abruptly on a day like this! Plague! That would have been nice. (a rap on the street door) Who's that? (looking through the peephole in the door) The stranger I saw on the Pont Neuf today! Not handsome to begin with. A nose of unheard of length. And then—for Poquelin! That would be disaster if it comes to that. (more knocking) No! No! (the rapping gets harder, she considers) But the other one might hear. (deciding) Better to get rid of him. (going to the door)

CYRANO: (outside)

Ah, indeed! Are you going to open up for me?

MADELEINE:

Hey, there! Will you quiet down! You are making a racket.

CYRANO: (entering)

At last, I see you again, my goddess of tender charms. (going to her) A kiss right away. (she refuses her head) No. (stupidly) My name of Cyrano will be ruined! A kiss, quick!

MADELEINE: (her teeth on edge)

You were told no!

CYRANO:

That's what we shall see. And soon. (striding towards her) A feint, and straight for the enemy—

MADELEINE: (escaping from him and taking shelter behind the table)

Who puts herself out of range!

CYRANO:

Tricky wench! She intends to whet my appetite. Second assault. (readies to hurl himself on her; she stops him)

MADELEINE:

Indeed—Stop! (coming out from her retreat) I surrender, but of my own will. (he tries to embrace her; she recoils) Hold on! Understand that no one can take a kiss. A kiss is given. (blows him a kiss) There!

CYRANO: (nonplussed)

That's all?

MADELEINE: (firmly)

Now, if you please—out you go!

CYRANO:

And if I don't please?

MADELEINE:

Then it will always be this way! When Madeleine

Béjart puts a plan in her head, it's done immediately. Neither God, nor gallant can prevent it. (pointing to the door) What are you waiting for?

CYRANO:

I'm waiting until I feel like obeying you. For you've put me in the mood not to leave. It's very nice here, my darling! And can you imagine it's best to retreat on the verge of victory?

MADELEINE: (bursting out)

Victory? Ah, really, you deceive yourself with that mocking air, that outfit, that nose!

CYRANO: (vexed)

Then why did you open up for me?

MADELEINE:

In order to kick you out afterwards.

CYRANO:

And the kiss?

MADELEINE:

Given to be sooner rid of you. (very rude) And besides, you must understand by now without such a lengthy discussion that you are in the way.

CYRANO:

In the way?

MADELEINE:

You couldn't be more so! More than one can be! (a little annoyed and deciding) Wait. Push open that window.—What do you see?

CYRANO:

A tennis court.

MADELEINE:

And then—nothing else?

CYRANO: (looking on the other side)

Ah, over this way I see a theatre.

MADELEINE: (shutting the window on his nose)

Mine—which opens tomorrow to the public of the city. From that you will judge that it is very difficult for me, having a thousand tasks today and worries, to meditate long, sir, on your case. And when my troupe isn't even prepared to perform to waste an hour talking about a love affair.

CYRANO:

So, you do intend to kick me out?

MADELEINE:

I am quite sorry about it. (pushing him toward the door)

CYRANO: (aside)

Bah! So much the worse. The bitch is really very attractive. (turning abruptly, aloud) Once Cyrano successfully enters the door of a beauty, it takes a hundred men to make him leave. (flopping in an armchair) I shall not leave!

MADELEINE: (exasperated and going to the window)

The devil with this pigheaded character! (looking through the window) And Poquelin's finished!

CYRANO: (from his armchair)

My very dearest—

MADELEINE:

He'll kill himself!

CYRANO:

I adore the theatre.

MADELEINE:

He's coming up! (pointing to Cyrano) And this one's staying!

CYRANO:

You must love it, too?

MADELEINE:

Me? As for me, I detest you! (Cyrano shrugs his shoulders, smiling; she rushes to the door, aside) I prefer to be at a distance at the moment of contact! (she leaves)

CYRANO: (alone, hearing the door close)

Gone! (uproar at the door of the Tennis Court) And someone's coming. (pondering) The lover. If he's tactful, I will spare him. If not—! (touches his sword hilt) He won't have anything to laugh about. (strides about, hand on his sword, with his back to the door through which Poquelin enters)

POQUELIN: (aside)

A man here! In her place! (aloud, in a rough voice) Hey! Sir!

CYRANO: (stiffening at the tone but without turning, aside)

What's this mean?

POQUELIN: (more nervously)

What are you doing around here?

CYRANO: (with a furious air, but without turning)

What I please!

POQUELIN: (striding towards Cyrano, insolently)

Scoundrel!

CYRANO:

Damned insolent cuckold! (turning, drawing his sword)

POQUELIN: (recognizing him, dumbfounded)

Cyrano!

CYRANO: (also astounded)

Poquelin! A ghost!

POQUELIN:

Now then! Hurry, let me embrace you. (embracing him) Dear friend!

CYRANO:

Three years without seeing each other face to face. Have I changed since the days at Gassendi's?

POQUELIN:

No. Surely.

CYRANO:

And neither have you.

POQUELIN: (examining him)

First of all, ever bold!

CYRANO:

And as for you, with your soft and melancholy air— Have you seen Chapelle again?

POQUELIN: (as if distracted)

Rarely.

CYRANO:

And Bernier? Indeed—I recall—

POQUELIN: (interrupting him)

A word. By what chance—?

CYRANO:

Am I here? My dear friend—(stupidly) A woman—

POQUELIN: (violently)

And her name?

CYRANO: (astonished)

Damnation! With what an air you're speaking to me?

POQUELIN: (very passionately)

Her name, Cyrano, I beg you!

CYRANO: (hesitating now)

It's that—

POQUELIN: (frigidly)

Be discreet if you wish. I bet I know that name—La Béjart!

CYRANO: (betraying himself)

Who told you?

POQUELIN: (crushed, with sorrow)

It's her!

CYRANO: (running to him)

Ah! Poquelin. I'm only a cursed fool. You love her?

POQUELIN:

Alas!

CYRANO:

And you are suffering through her?

POQUELIN: (raging)

Infernal coquette!

CYRANO: (involuntarily approving)

Ah, indeed! The young lady can boast of being one! (returning to the situation) All the same, calm down. This is the first time I've entered her roof—on honor!

POQUELIN:

Eh! What do I care!

CYRANO:

And what's more, I must tell you. She kicked me out.

POQUELIN: (with sad irony)

So I see!

CYRANO:

Everything conspires to wrong me. And, truly, I had these wrongs for myself alone.

POQUELIN: (stopping him)

Useless, friend, all your efforts are superfluous. I see that she is incorrigible. And that she lied to me. It's no longer possible for me to live here any longer, I'm leaving.

CYRANO:

I am in despair.

POQUELIN:

Why—you found yourself there without knowing. You or some one else. It's the same score. She no longer loves me—and I'm leaving.

CYRANO:

But they tell about these things—Nothing happened.

POQUELIN: (very grave)

I'm still leaving.

CYRANO: (also grave)

It's serious—?

POQUELIN:

Yes, certainly. (a pause)

CYRANO:

Perhaps it's better. After all—A wise proverb says "Far from the eyes, far from the heart". By being courageous today, friend, your pain will sooner flee. I am certain of it. And one fine morning, I bet you will awake content, free and cured. On that—time's wasting. At the Pine Cone they must be making a feast. Come!

(Through the window an uproar from the rehearsal. Poquelin, about to follow Cyrano, suddenly stops.)

POQUELIN:

One moment.

CYRANO:

What for?

POQUELIN: (in an emotional voice)

That applause!

CYRANO:

What are those bravos to you? (more applause)

POQUELIN: (aside)

Again! At every moment! (dragging Cyrano towards the window) Look. Béjart's playing. And everyone in the hall's applauding. Indeed, the scene is without equal! (carried away, applauding in his turn) Ah! Bravo! Comrade!

CYRANO: (watching him, astonished)

Huh? Comrade? Eh, what! Comrades—these folk?

POQUELIN:

They are what I am—it's true. To follow Madeleine, I became an actor.

CYRANO:

You go on the stage?

POQUELIN: (with melancholy)

I won't do it anymore. My dream's destroyed—That applause! Those bravos! Ah! that uproar—(passionately, with increasing excitement) No! You cannot know, Cyrano, what intoxication one feels when: ceaselessly bursting on the ear, growling like thunder and gripping you by the heart this uproar teaches you that you are the conqueror in the battle joined for the soul of men. That this is ours, small as we are, for, according to how it pleased us to transfigure it, we've made it smile or we've made it weep! To see, at a short distance away, like a big dark hole, all those human creatures who appear numberless, living in a lightning flash the life we determine, impassioned with our passion, burning with our fires, pained with our pain and mad with our joy. Molding them at our whim, made into our prey. And then to hear them, like a wave on the sea whose murmur rises and increases in the air. To bless with both their hands the magic gift, which revealed for one instant, ravishes them for their life. This great and exquisite time, that I, yes, I have known that escapes you. Alas, I will never see it again!

CYRANO:

What passion defending a situation that has, I admit, its pleasures and its pride. But when one acts, mustn't you reckon with bad days?

POQUELIN:

If Paris greets me ill, the provinces always remain to me.

CYRANO:

Wandering from village to village!

POQUELIN:

And what do I care about that long pilgrimage if I see endlessly appearing at the end of the road, after the somber present, a bright tomorrow! (becoming heated again) And even if this dawn never shines, even in despair I would still hope. Because I would have in my heart a divine cordial warming my misery with the fire of the ideal! (pause, falling back into a reverie) But, at present—(remaining pensive, he goes toward the trunk into which he threw his books)

CYRANO: (aside)

And still nothing about his mistress. It's abandoning his art that causes his distress. He must remain! (watching Poquelin rummaging in the trunk) But—What are you looking for in there?

POQUELIN:

Don't bother me. (going to the chimney)

CYRANO:

But I want to see that. Those papers—are you going to burn them?

POQUELIN: (evasively)

Absurd gibberish.

CYRANO: (jestingly)

Carefully hidden in the depths of a closet? Then, you're an author? May one see your work? (extending his hand) Give it to me.

POQUELIN:

Why, no.

CYRANO:

Very fine! (grabs them by surprise) I've got it—We'll read this in detail. (putting it in his pocket)

POQUELIN:

They're only formless essays. Return them to me.

CYRANO: (pulling them out of his pocket)

Then let's have a look at this enormous stupidity. (leafing through them and reading the titles) Gorgibus in the Bag. The Amorous Doctor. The Fagot-Makers—good—good—The Pedant—(stopping) Nice title. (negligently) As for me, I used that title for a comedy that I wrote in verse about philosophy.

POQUELIN: (smiling)

I remember it quite well. The story of Granger. An excellent morsel that I dared to copy. (showing him a page) There!

CYRANO: (looking)

That's right! (reading) "What's he come to do in this gallery?" (threatening him as a joke) Behold this author who pillages his colleagues.

POQUELIN: (most serious)

Yes, I was a born pillager.

CYRANO: (excitedly)

But I'm not angry with you for having taken a grain of salt from my poor meal!

POQUELIN: (pensively)

To pillage. (to Cyrano) Open these notes at random. Take the trouble to view these fragments carved out by the handful from the homes of these times and from antiquity, and amongst the French, on the one hand, and Spain and Italy on the other. (leafing himself) Here—this is from Terence; that's from Plautus. A character trait here, this from the Florentine farces—further on, this is an extract from an old Medieval tale. On this other page a word culled from our stage. Did I plunder enough of them all in the course of reading? And I have no remorse, I assure you for having pillaged wherever my treasure was to be found!

CYRANO: (smiling)

Your "treasure"—Since—

POQUELIN:

Since I make it mine! Because whatever is old rejuvenates quickly through contact with another soul and casts out a new flame. Because all my larcenies in their turn become law! Because under the borrowed mask I am ME!

CYRANO:

But to be original is a difficult thing. Everything's been done down here. You must be docile and follow the scent on every track to the end. Or—do like me. When I have enough of this old world, I will seek my fortune in the Sun and find talent in the Moon!

POQUELIN:

To my way of thinking, Cyrano, no one needs to seek talent either so high or so low. And one need only cast his eyes on this earth to find subjects to know what to make of them. Life is a great book in which one has only to peer and there you can see everything, then use it later.

CYRANO:

But one sees so little—

POQUELIN:

The whole trick is to observe the little one sees. And then to hold it in reserve. These accumulated nothings later form a body, a living body.

CYRANO: (doubtfully)

Living? Through the power of art!

POQUELIN: (firmly)

Living because made from life. All that I perceive about me. I feel inclined to engrave in my head—swiftly, like a thief hiding gold under his cloak. Vice, virtue, despair, joy. It must all be stolen from passersby who one jostles. Coquettes scorning in whispers behind a fan; those whose too frank love is a scandal; the miser loving his money almost to a frenzy; false devotees trapped in their hypocrisy. In the end, all that you, I, or anyone can see. And must have seen; and clearly seen to know in what direction the world turns and who peoples it. Tomorrow as today; it's human baseness. And do you think that by pursuing that; by fixing all these characteristics without being pedantic, without passing sentence, doing nothing except revealing Mankind to the credulous theatre what is in life, either vile or ridiculous, you haven't done something better than being original because one has done good by pointing out what is bad! (a pause, then sadly) Ah, Cyrano, doubtless you laugh and that's justice! To hear these big words on the subject of a rough draft or two of no importance, one or two sketches of farces, Gorgibus, The Fagot-makers! You are going to take me for a dummy who's done nothing, in short, and talks to you in the manner of an oracle and as a great man. You'll say to yourself—

CYRANO:

I was saying to myself that to count on the future is a useless worry. A world may end because of an errant atom off its course. But that if one must triumph over this doubt, if one can predict to someone that that person will be great some day, and thereafter will belong to us first and that afterwards the thoughts he reveals and the words he speaks and through the new soul that one feels hatching within—it will surely be to you that, forgetting that chance rules, one will say "I am certain of your future glory. You will be great. Your name is one of those that the voice of great destinies already murmurs and that humanity will repeat morning and night—" (slowly) Now that was my thought. (a short pause) I was also thinking that your soul, injured by a pain of love will receive its cure without your being forced to leave the house where I feel the voice of the future is calling you.

POQUELIN: (excitedly)

No. The deception was far too cruel. To love without being loved. I want to leave forever, without delay. I am thirsty to escape from this love.

CYRANO:

You have only that dream in the world?

POQUELIN:

Yes, I am capable of desiring glory without playing second fiddle. What you were promising me just now. Tonight, when everyone slept, that deceitful dream was able to boast to me, as sweetly as when one emerges from childhood; when one is full of noble confidences—to become one day—who knows? A great actor and who knows—even?—who knows? more, much more an author! That was too beautiful. Let's be, like Papa Poquelin an upholsterer, but not as good. This is the end of Molière, a poor and costly adopted name!

CYRANO:

Molière. A perfect name and one that must protect you.

POQUELIN:

The sacrifice has been made. (going toward the street door) Are you coming?

CYRANO: (searching for a way to retain him)

To leave! To leave! (finding one) But first of all, I

think—have you the right to leave so carelessly? I would think it ill done to leave so emotionlessly these folks, these fine people who, all of them, are counting on you.

POQUELIN: (shaken)

My comrades—

CYRANO:

Yes. After promising to be with them, in fortune or in distress, the leader who protects them, the friend who sustains them, the one who doesn't flee when misfortune occurs?

POQUELIN: (in a very low voice)

That was me!

CYRANO:

You see!

POQUELIN: (pondering)

Yes, yes—It would be cowardly to leave them with the work. (coming to himself) But this love affair is still odious to me.

CYRANO:

Ingrate! Your love? When it's she—yes, she, who wants you to be great. And this Madeleine that you curse—it's the perfume of her breath, and the gold of her hair, and the luster of her complexion, which wants an illustrious destiny for you, since she culled you as you followed your obscure path, to throw you into the arms of your future glory, and she was the good luck, the holy opportunity who conquered your vocation for you, ingrate!

POQUELIN:

Did she have to uproot me like a weed?

CYRANO:

Suffering is at times a leaven of hope. And when one wants, as you do, to depict misfortunes, which are from earthly kings to serfs in hamlets, humanity's eternal pasturage—it's not enough to see them on the page of a book, and to have observed suffering in the abstract. It's better they are felt in the flesh. And that the dying heart can say of itself to others, "These ills were mine before being yours."

POQUELIN:

You say the truth. As for this love, indeed, either I'll cure myself of it or I must suffer from it. Well, I will suffer, but I will remain here, friend. (extending his hand to him)

MADELEINE: (reentering quietly, aside)

Good friends! What a piece of luck! As for me, I was expecting to see them butcher each other. (as she comes forward the two men notice her)

POQUELIN:

Madeleine, your invented admirer has almost converted me.

MADELEINE: (delighted)

Really? Not jealous anymore?

POQUELIN: (with a sad smile)

At least I haven't left!

MADELEINE:

In that case, no longer lovers—huh? But good comrades. (she offers her hand to Poquelin who takes it)

POQUELIN: (to Cyrano)

This ends all the rows. (pointing to himself) The lover—(carefully seeking for his word) Unlucky, beaten, but content!

MADELEINE:

Hell! Tomorrow there will be a dazzling success. (to Cyrano) Indeed, sir, since you are his crony—(pointing to Poquelin) you will come to applaud Poquelin?

CYRANO: (gravely, raising his hat)

No—Molière!

CURTAIN

THE LOVE DOCTOR
by Molière

CAST OF CHARACTERS

Sganarelle (father of Lucinda) (Molière)

Lucinda

Clitandre (lover to Lucinda)

Lucrèce (cousin of Sganarelle)

Lisette (Lucinda's servant)

Aminte (neighbor of Sganarelle)

Mr. Guillame (a seller of tapestry)

Mr. Josse

Dr. Tomes

Dr. Des Fernandes

Dr. Macroton

Dr. Bahays

Mr. Filerin

A Notary

Champagne (Sganarelle's valet)

Comedy

Music

Ballet

PROLOGUE

COMEDY

Leave, leave our vain quarrel. Let's not dispute our talents one after the other. And of a greater glory pride ourselves today Let's all three write in a passion without equal To give pleasure to the greatest king in the world.

COMEDY, MUSIC BALLET

Let's all three unite in a passion without equal. To give pleasure to the greatest king in the world.

COMEDY

From his deeds, greater than can be believed. He sometimes comes to relax among us.

Is there greater glory?

Is there sweeter happiness?

COMEDY, MUSIC BALLET

Let's all three unite in a passion without equal. To give pleasure to the greatest king in the world.

ACT I

SGANARELLE

Ah—what a strange thing life is and how I can indeed say with that great philosopher of antiquity that he who has money has troubles and that no misfortune ever comes without another! I had only one wife—who died.

MR. GUILLAME

And how many do you want to have?

SGANARELLE

She died my friend. That loss is very painful to me, and I cannot think back on it without weeping. I wasn't very satisfied with her conduct—and we often quarreled with each other, but still, death puts all things to right. She's dead; I weep for her. If she were in life, we would be quarrelling. Of all the children that heaven gave me, it left me only one daughter, and that daughter is all my trouble for I see her in the most somber melancholy in the world in a dreadful sadness whose cause I don't even know and there seems no way of extracting her from it. As for me, I'm losing my wits and I need good advice on this matter.

(to Lucrèce) You are my niece.

(to Aminte) You are my neighbor.

(to Mr. Guillame and Mr. Josse) And you, my pals, and my friends—I beg you to advise me all that I must do.

MR. JOSSE

As for me, I hold that finery and fancy dress are the thing which most rejoice girls—and if I were like you, I would buy for her, as of today a beautiful ornament of diamonds, rubies or emeralds.

MR. GUILLAME

And I, if I was in your place, I would purchase a beautiful hanging tapestry of forest scenery or characters that I would put in her room to rejuvenate her spirit and sight.

AMINTE

For myself, I wouldn't do much that way—and I would marry her very quickly and the quickest way I could—with this person who you got for her, they say, ask if there is time.

LUCRÈCE

And as for me, I hold that your daughter is not at all fit for marriage. She has a very delicate complexion and not very healthy and it would be a determination to send her soon to the other world by exposing her, the way she is—to having children. The world is not at all her thing—and I advise you to put her in a convent—where she will find diversions more in accord with her humor—

SGANARELLE

All this advice is assuredly admirable but I hold them a little biased and find that you advise me quite well for yourselves. You are in the business, Mr. Josse, and your advice smells of a man who wants to rid himself of his stock in trade.

You sell tapestries, Mr. Guillame and you have the look of having some hanging that inconveniences you. The one you love, dear cousin, is rumored to have some inclination to my daughter, and you wouldn't be annoyed to see her married to someone else. As for you, my dear niece, it's not my plan to marry my daughter with just anybody—and I have my reasons for that—but the advice you give me to make her a nun is from a woman who indeed might charitably wish to be my sole heir. So, gentlemen and ladies, although your advice may be the best in the world—you'll understand, if you please, why I am not following it.

(All leave except Sganarelle.)

SGANARELLE

So there go my fashionable advice givers.

(Lucinda enters.)

SGANARELLE

Ah, there's my daughter taking the air—she doesn't see me. She's sighing—she's raising her eyes to heaven.

(to Lucinda) May God protect you! Hello, my darling. Hey there! What is it? How are you doing—? Alas, always sad and melancholy like this—and you don't want to tell me what's wrong—? Come on—open your little heart to me. There, my poor darling, to me. There, my poor darling, tell, tell all your little thoughts—to your little papa—pretty. Courage! Do you want me to kiss you? Come on!

(aside) I'm furious to see her in this mood—

(to Lucinda) But talk to me—do you want to make me die of annoyance—can't I know where this great languor comes from? Tell me the cause and I promise I will do everything for you—yes, you only need to tell me the subject of your sadness; I assure you here, and promise you, there is nothing I won't do to satisfy you—it's only to be said—are you jealous of one of your companions that you see better dressed than you?

Is there some new material you want to have a dress made out of? No. Is your room not fancy enough and you want some closet—from the fair at Saint Laurent? That's not it—do you want to learn something and you want me to give you a teacher who will show you how to play the harpsichord? Nope. Are you in love with someone and you'd like to get married?

(Lucinda makes an affirmative sign, Lisette enters)

LISETTE

Well, sir—you've just had a conversation with your daughter—have you discovered this cause of this melancholy?

SGANARELLE

No—she's a slut who infuriates me.

LISETTE

Sir—let me do it—I'm going to sound her out a little.

SGANARELLE

It's not necessary—and since she wants to be in the mood, I'm of the opinion to leave her there—

LISETTE

Let me do it, I tell you. Perhaps she'll disclose herself

more freely to me than to you. What! Madame—you don't tell us what's wrong with you—and you want to afflict everyone this way—? It seems to me that one doesn't act the way you are doing—and that if you have some reluctance to explain yourself to your father, you ought not to have any to disclosing your feelings to me. Tell me—do you want something from him? He's told us many times that he would spare nothing to satisfy you. Aren't you given all the freedom you want? And the gifts and the walls—don't they engage your soul's attention? What! Have you received some insult from someone? When! Don't you have some secret inclination that you want your father to marry you to? Ah—I understand you, that's the thing! What the Devil! Why so many names? Sir, the mystery is solved and—

SGANARELLE

Go ungrateful daughter—I don't want to speak to you anymore and I leave you in your obstinacy—

LUCINDA

Father, since you really want me to tell you this thing—

SGANARELLE

Yes, I am losing the friendship that I had for you.

LISETTE

Sir, her sadness—

SGANARELLE

She's a slut who wants to make me die—

LUCINDA

Father, I really want—

SGANARELLE

This is the reward I get for raising you the way I have—

LISETTE

But, sir—

SGANARELLE

No—I'm against her in a terrible rage.

LUCINDA

But father—

SGANARELLE

I no longer have any tenderness for you.

LISETTE

But—

SGANARELLE

She's a bitch.

LUCINDA

But—

SGANARELLE

An ingrate.

LISETTE

But—

SGANARELLE

A slut who won't tell me what's the matter with her.

LISETTE

It's a husband she wants.

SGANARELLE

(pretending not to understand her) I abandon her—

LISETTE

A husband.

SGANARELLE

I detest her—

LISETTE

A husband.

SGANARELLE

And I renounce her as my daughter.

LISETTE

A husband.

SGANARELLE

Don't even talk to me about her anymore.

LISETTE

A husband.

SGANARELLE

Don't speak to me about her anymore. (he exits)

LISETTE

A husband, a husband, a husband.

They say truly there is no one more deaf than those

who don't want to hear.

LUCINDA

Alas, Lisette—I was wrong to hide my unhappiness—and I had only to speak to have whatever I wanted from my father! You see him.

LISETTE

On my oath—he's a villainous man—and I admit to you it would give me extreme pleasure to play him some trick—but why does it come about, Madame, that up to now you've hidden your illness from me—

LUCINDA

Alas! What would have been the use in discovering it to you sooner? And wouldn't I have been better off hiding it all my life? Do you think I have not foreseen all you see now, that I didn't probe to the depths all my father's feelings—and that the refusal that he gave to the one who asked for me through a friend, didn't choke every sort of hope in my heart?

LISETTE

What! It's this stranger who asked for you?

LUCINDA

Perhaps it's not right for a girl to explain herself so

freely, but still I confess to you that if I were permitted to desire something—this would be what I want. We've had no conversation together—and his mouth has not declared the passion that he has for me—but in all the places that he was able to see me—his looks and his actions have always spoken so tenderly and the request he made for me seemed to me that of such an honest man that my heart couldn't prevent itself from being sensible of his ardor—and how the hardness of my father has reduced all this tenderness.

LISETTE

Go—let me do it. Whatever complaint I may have about your secrecy from me, I don't want to forego assisting you in your love affair—and since you have enough courage—

LUCINDA

But what do you expect me to do against a father's authority—? And if he is inexorable to my prayers?

LISETTE

Go, go—it's not necessary to let oneself be led like a ninny so long as honor isn't offended—one can free oneself a little from the tyranny of a father. What's he pretend you are doing? Aren't you of an age to be married?

And does he think you're made of marble? Go, one more thing—I want to serve your passion—from now on, I take on myself the care of his interests and you will see I know some tricks—but I see your father—let's go back in and allow me to act.

(The women leave Sganarelle)

SGANARELLE

Sometimes it's good not to seem to hear things one hears only too well—and I've wisely been spared the declaration of a desire I am not resolved to satisfy. Has there ever been seen a greater tyranny than this custom they want to impose on fathers, nothing more impertinent and more ridiculous than to amass wealth with great work and to raise a daughter with great care and tenderness to be despoiled of both by the hands of a man who pays us nothing? No, no—I mock that custom and I intend to keep my wealth and my daughter for myself.

LISETTE

(running around the stage and pretending not to see Sganarelle) Ah—misfortune, ah, disgrace! Ah, poor Mr. Sganarelle—where shall I find you?

SGANARELLE

(aside) What's she saying?

LISETTE

(still running) Ah! Wretched father! What will you do when you learn this news?

SGANARELLE

(aside) What can it be?

LISETTE

My poor mistress.

SGANARELLE

(aside) I am ruined.

LISETTE

Ah—

SGANARELLE

(running after Lisette) Lisette.

LISETTE

What misfortune!

SGANARELLE

Lisette.

LISETTE

What an accident.

SGANARELLE

Lisette.

LISETTE

What fatality.

SGANARELLE

Lisette.

LISETTE

(stopping) Ah! Sir!

SGANARELLE

What is it?

LISETTE

Sir.

SGANARELLE

What's wrong—

LISETTE

Your daughter—

SGANARELLE

Ah! Ah!

LISETTE

Sir, don't cry like that, for you'll make me laugh.

SGANARELLE

Speak quickly then.

LISETTE

Your daughter—completely taken by the words you said to her and by the terrifying rage she saw you in against her and full of despair—opened the window which looks on the river—

SGANARELLE

So!

LISETTE

Then, raising her eyes to heaven—"No," she said, "it is impossible to live with the wrath of my father—and since he renounces me as his daughter—I intend to die."

SGANARELLE

And she threw herself in?

LISETTE

No sir, she shut the window quietly, and went to put herself on her bed. There she took to crying bitterly, and suddenly her face went pale, her eyes turned, her heart failed her and she remained like that in my arms.

SGANARELLE

Ah—my daughter!

LISETTE

By means of torturing her, I made her come to her self, but this thing takes her back moment by moment, and I think she won't last the day.

SGANARELLE

Champagne! Champagne! Champagne! Quickly, find me some doctors and in quantity. Can't have too many in such a situation. Ah, my daughter, my only daughter—

FIRST INTERLUDE

Champagne, Sganarelle's valet dances to the door of four doctors. The four doctors dance and ceremoniously go into Sganarelle's house.

ACT II

LISETTE

Sir, what do you intend to do with four doctors? Isn't one enough to kill a person?

SGANARELLE

Be quiet. Four opinions are better than one.

LISETTE

Can't your daughter die without the help of these gentleman here?

SGANARELLE

Do doctors cause death?

LISETTE

Doubtless and I knew a man who could prove it with good reasons—so you never had to say—such and such a person died of fever and the flux in the breast, but "she died of four doctors and two pharmacists".

SGANARELLE

Hush! Don't offend these gentlemen.

LISETTE

My word, sir, our cat survived a jump from the roof of a house to a street, and it went 3 days without eating and it couldn't move foot or paw—but it was really lucky there were no cat doctors, for her affair would have been done—and they wouldn't have failed to purge and bleed her.

SGANARELLE

Will you shut up? I tell you. But look what impudence! Here they are.

LISETTE

Take care, you're really going to be edified. They're going to tell you in Latin that your daughter is sick.

(Enter Doctors Tomes, Des Fernandes, Macroton and Bahays)

SGANARELLE

Well, gentlemen?

DOCTOR TOMES

We've seen the patient sufficiently and there is no doubt, she's full of impurities.

DOCTOR TOMES

I mean that there are many impurities in her body—a number of corrupted humors.

SGANARELLE

Ah. I understand you.

DOCTOR TOMES

But—we are going to consult together.

SGANARELLE

Come—get them chairs—

LISETTE

(to Dr. Tomes) Ah, sir, you are involved!

SGANARELLE

(to Lisette) How do you know this gentleman?

LISETTE

From having seen him the other day at the home of a

good friend of your niece's.

DOCTOR TOMES

How's her coachman doing?

LISETTE

Fine. He's dead.

DOCTOR TOMES

Dead?

LISETTE

Yes.

DOCTOR TOMES

That cannot be.

LISETTE

I don't know if it can be—but I know quite well he's dead.

DOCTOR TOMES

He cannot be dead, I tell you.

LISETTE

And as for me, I tell you he's dead and buried.

DOCTOR TOMES

You are mistaken.

LISETTE

I saw the funeral.

DOCTOR TOMES

That is impossible. Hippocrates says that this sort of illness doesn't terminate in less than fourteen or more than twenty-one days—and he only fell ill six days ago.

LISETTE

Hippocrates can say what he pleases—but her coachman is dead.

SGANARELLE

Peace—argumentation! Come one, let's get out of here. Gentlemen, I beg you to consult in the best way. Although it is not the custom to pay in advance—sometimes, for fear of forgetting—and so it may be taken care of—here—(giving each money and receiving from each a different gesture in return)

(The doctors sit down and cough)

DR. des FERNANDES

Paris is strangely large and it's necessary to make long treks when business requires.

DOCTOR TOMES

I have to confess I have an admirable mule for that, and you'd hardly believe the work I get out of him every day.

DR. des FERNANDES

I have a marvelous horse and he's a tireless animal.

DOCTOR TOMES

Do you know the road my mule took today? First, I went by the Arsenal—from the Arsenal to the middle of Faubourg Saint Germain to the end of the Marais—from the end of the Marais to Port Saint Honore—from Port Saint Honoré to Faubourg St. Jacques, from St. Jacques to the Porte Richelieu, from the Porte Richelieu to here—and from here, I've got to go again to the Place Royale.

DR. des FERNANDES

My horse has done all that today—and moreover I've been to Ruel to see a patient.

DOCTOR TOMES

But by the way—what side are you taking in the quarrel between the two doctors, Theoplurastus and Artemius? For it's an affair dividing our whole association.

DR. des FERNANDES

As for me, I am for Artemius.

DOCTOR TOMES

And me too. It's not that his opinion, as has been seen, didn't kill the patient—and that of Theoplurastus was not much better—assuredly—but still, he was wrong in the circumstances—and he ought not to be of an opinion different from his elder—what do you say about it?

DR. des FERNANDES

Doubtless. One must always preserve the formalities whatever may happen.

DOCTOR TOMES

As for me, I am devilishly strict, at least, so long as it's between friends—and they brought us together one day—three of us—with a doctor from elsewhere—for a consultation. But I stopped the whole business and wouldn't endure anyone giving an opinion if things weren't going to be in order—the people of the house did what they could—and the illness pressed on—but I didn't want to give up—and the patient died bravely during this argument.

DR. des FERNANDES

It's very well to teach people to live and show them how dumb they are.

DOCTOR TOMES

A man dead is only a dead man and there are no consequences—but a formality neglected brings a notable prejudice to medicine itself.

SGANARELLE

(entering) Gentlemen, my daughter's suffering is getting worse—I beg you to tell me quickly what you have decided.

DOCTOR TOMES

Go ahead, sir—

DR. des FERNANDES

No, sir—speak, if you please.

DOCTOR TOMES

You are mocking—

DR. des FERNANDES

I shall not speak first.

DOCTOR TOMES

Sir.

DR. des FERNANDES

Sir.

SGANARELLE

Hey—merry gentlemen, leave all these ceremonies and think that things are pressing.

(They all four speak at once)

DOCTOR TOMES

The illness of your daughter—

DR. des FERNANDES

The opinion of all these gentlemen together.

DR. MACROTON

After careful consultation—

DR. BAHAYS

To reason—

SGANARELLE

Hey, gentlemen, speak one after the other—mercy—

DOCTOR TOMES

Sir, we've considered your daughter's illness, and my opinion is that it proceeds from a great heat in the blood—thus, I conclude to bleed her as soon as you can.

DR. des FERNANDES

As for me, I say that her illness is a mixture of humors caused by too much eating, so I conclude to give her an emetic.

DOCTOR TOMES

I contend that an emetic will kill her.

DR. des FERNANDES

And I that bleeding will kill her.

DOCTOR TOMES

Really, just to make yourself look clever.

DR. des FERNANDES

Yes, that's my opinion and I will lend you the crown in all types of erudition.

DOCTOR TOMES

Do you recall the man you caused to croak a few days ago?

DR. des FERNANDES

Do you remember the lady you sent to the next world three days ago?

DOCTOR TOMES

(to Sganarelle) I've told you my opinion.

DR. des FERNANDES

(to Sganarelle) I've told you my ideas.

DOCTOR TOMES

If you don't bleed your daughter right away, she's a dead person.

(he leaves)

DR. des FERNANDES

If you do bleed her, she won't live more than a quarter of an hour.

(he leaves)

SGANARELLE

Which of the two to believe? And what decision to take on such opposed opinions. Gentlemen, I conjure you to convince me and tell me without passion what you think is the most proper thing to treat my daughter.

DR. MACROTON

Sir—in these matters, one must proceed slowly and with circumspection, and do nothing, as they say—on the fly—the worst fault one can do is to cause dangerous consequences, according to our master Hippocrates.

DR. BAHAYS

It's true one must be careful what one does—for this is not child's play here—and when one fails, it's not easy to repair the fault and to reestablish what one has ruined, experiment cautiously—that's what, it's a case of reasoning above all—of weighing things carefully—of considering the temperament of people—of examining the causes of the illness and of seeing the remedies one can bring to it.

SGANARELLE

(aside) The one tortures it—and the other runs the post.

DR. MACROTON

Then, sir, to come to the point, I find that your daughter has a chronic illness and that she can be at risk if she doesn't get help—moreover, the symptoms that she has are indicative of a sooty and corrosive vapor, which dot the membranes of her brain. Now this vapor, that we call in Greek atmos, is caused by putrid humors which are tenacious and congultinuous and have their origin in the lower bowels.

DR. BAHAYS

And as these humors have been engendered over a long period of time they've reheated themselves and have acquired this malignity which steam towards the region of the brain.

DR. MACROTON

So, indeed, then to draw out, detach, remove, expel, evacuate, the aforesaid humors—there must be a vigorous purgation—but before going any further, I find it relevant and it wouldn't be inconvenient to use small palatives—remedies, meaning little soft enemas and cleansing of julep and refreshing syrups that one can mix in her tea.

DR. BAHAYS

Then we will come to the purging—and the bleeding, which we will repeat if need be.

DR. MACROTON

It's not that with all this your daughter may not die—but at least you will have done something and have the consolation of knowing that she died properly.

DR. BAHAYS

It's better to die according to the rules than to escape despite the rules.

DR. MACROTON

We have told you our thoughts sincerely.

DR. BAHAYS

And we've spoken to you as we would speak to our own brother.

SGANARELLE

(to Macroton and stretching his words) I render you very humble. Thanks. (to Dr. Bahays stammering) And you are infinitely obliged by the trouble you have taken.

(the two doctors leave) Here I am now a little more uncertain than I was before. The devil! A fantasy has come to me. I have to go buy some snake oil and make her take it—snake oil is a remedy which many people are very fond of. Hola!

(Scene is now street)

SGANARELLE

Hola! Sir—I beg you give me a bottle of your snake oil which I will pay you for.

OPERATOR

(singing) Can all the gold of all the climbs that surround the ocean ever pay for this important secret? My remedy cures through its rare excellence—more ills than you can count in a year.

OPERATOR

The Itch

Scabs, scurvy

Fever

Plague

Gout, syphilis

Measles

and stooping. Oh the tremendous power of snake oil.

SGANARELLE

Sir, I believe that all the gold in the world is not capable of paying for your remedy—but still here's a thirty-sous coin for you to take if you please.

OPERATOR

(singing) Admire my snake oil and with the little I sell you—this treasure my hand dispenses to you—you can brave with assurance all the ills which the wrath of heaven pours on us.

The Itch

Scabs, scurvy

Fever

Plague

Gout, syphilis

Measles

and stooping. Oh the great power of snake oil.

SECOND INTERMISSION

Several travelers and several Scaramouches, valets of the operator rejoice in dancing.

ACT III

DOCTOR FILERIN

Aren't you ashamed, gentlemen, to display so little prudence for people of your age and for you to be quarrelling like young dolts. Don't you see what evil these sorts of quarrels do us in the world? And isn't it enough that scientists are aware of the contradictions and dissensions that exist between our authorities and our ancient masters, without revealing to people through our arguments and our quarrels the bravado of our art. As for me, I don't understand at all this master scheming of some of our folks and it is necessary to admit that all these arguments have discredited us in a strange manner and that if we aren't careful we are going to ruin ourselves.

I'm not speaking only for my interest, for thank God, I'm very well off—let it snow, let it pour, let it hail. Those who are dead are dead and I have somewhat to spend with the livery—but in the end all these disputes are not good for medicine.

Since heaven has graced us for many centuries people

remain infatuated with us—let's not disabuse people with our extravagant cliques and let's profit by their stupidity as softly as we can.

We are not the only ones, you know, who try to prevail on human weakness. Most of the world studies that and each is forced to take men by their weakness to extract some profit. Flatterers, for example, seek to profit from the love men have to be praised by giving them all the vain flattering they wish and what they do is an act—which can be seen from their considerable fortunes. The alchemists try to profit from the passion for riches by promising mountains of gold to those who listen to them. And the tellers of horoscopes, by their deceitful predictions, profit from the vanity and ambition of credulous spirits. But the greatest weakness of men is the love they have for living and we profit from it, by our pompous bombast and know how to use to our advantage this veneration that the fear of death gives to our profession. Let us preserve the degree of esteem that their weakness places in us and be in concert around the patients to attribute to ourselves the happy outcome of the illness and to cast on nature the blunders of our art. Let's not, I say to you, stupidly destroy the fortunate bias by an error which gives bread to so many people.

DOCTOR TOMES

You are correct in all that you say—but there are heats of blood which sometimes one is not the master.

DOCTOR FILERIN

Come then, gentlemen, put aside your rancor and let's reach your settlement here.

DOCTOR des FERNANDES

I agree. Just let me give my emetic for the patient that needs it and I will let him do whatever he wants to the first patient he's involved with.

DOCTOR FILERIN

One couldn't speak more fairly and that's how to set things straight.

DR. des FERNANDES

That's done.

DOCTOR FILERIN

Put it there—goodbye. Another time, show more prudence.

(Exit Filerin.)

LISETTE

(enters) What! There you are, gentlemen, and you are not thinking of repairing the wrong done to medicine.

DOCTOR TOMES

What do you mean? What is it?

LISETTE

An insolent who had the effrontery to encroach on your profession and without your orders has just killed a man by running him through with a sword.

DOCTOR TOMES

Listen, you play the mocker but you'll fall into our hands some day—

LISETTE

I'll let you kill me if ever I have recourse to you.

(The doctors leave)

CLITANDRE

(entering dressed like a doctor) Well, Lisette—do you like me like this?

LISETTE

The best in the world and I've been waiting for you impatiently, anyway, nature made me the most humane person in the world and I cannot see two lovers sigh for each other without falling into a charitable tenderness and an ardent desire to assuage the pain they suffer. I intend at any price to extract Lucinda from the tyranny she is under and to put her in your power—you pleased me from the first and I know people and she cannot make a better choice.

Love risks extraordinary things and we have agreed together on a sort of stratagem which perhaps will succeed for us. All our measures have been taken already. The man we're dealing with is not the cleverest fellow in this world—and if this adventure fails us, we will find a thousand other ways—to arrive at our end. Wait for me there, alone, and I'll return to fetch you.

(Clitandre retires to the back of the stage)

LISETTE

Sir! Hallelujah! Hallelujah!

SGANARELLE

What is it?

LISETTE

Rejoice!

SGANARELLE

About what?

LISETTE

Rejoice, I tell you.

SGANARELLE

Tell me what it is and then perhaps I'll rejoice.

LISETTE

No—I want you to rejoice beforehand—so you'll sing and dance.

SGANARELLE

Over what?

LISETTE

On my word—

SGANARELLE

All right.

(he sings and dances) La, la, la—what the devil!

LISETTE

Sir, your daughter is cured.

SGANARELLE

My daughter is cured!

LISETTE

Yes, I am bringing you a doctor, but a doctor of importance, who makes marvelous cures and who mocks other doctors.

SGANARELLE

Where is he?

LISETTE

I'm going to bring him in.

(goes out)

SGANARELLE

We'll have to see if this one is better than the others.

LISETTE

(returning with Clitandre) Here he is.

SGANARELLE

Here's a doctor with a really fresh beard.

LISETTE

Science doesn't measure itself by the beard—and it's not by the chin that he is skillful.

SGANARELLE

Sir, they tell me that you have admirable remedies to evacuate the bowels.

CLITANDRE

Sir, my remedies are different from those of others. They have emetics, bleedings, pills and enemas, but me, I cure with words, with sounds, with letters—with talismans and with rings made under the influence of constellations.

LISETTE

What did I tell you?

SGANARELLE

Here's a great man.

LISETTE

Sir, as your daughter is all dressed in a chair, I am going to make her come here.

SGANARELLE

Yes, do that.

CLITANDRE

(taking Sganarelle's pulse) Your daughter is really sick.

SGANARELLE

You know that here?

CLITANDRE

Yes, from the sympathy there is between father and daughter.

LISETTE

(bringing Lucinda)

(to Clitandre) Here sir, there's a chair beside her.

(to Sganarelle) Come, let's leave them together.

SGANARELLE

Why, I want to remain here.

LISETTE

You're looking? We have to separate. A doctor has a hundred things to ask that it isn't right for a man to hear.

(Sganarelle and Lisette move away.)

CLITANDRE

(low to Lucinda) Ah, Madame, how great is the rapture in which I find myself. And how little I know how to begin speaking to you! Up to now I've spoken to you only with my eyes—I had, so it seemed to me, a hundred things to say—and now that I have the liberty of speaking to you in the manner I wish—I remain dumbfounded and the great joy I am in chokes off my words.

LUCINDA

I can tell you the same thing and I feel, like you, emotions of joy which prevent me from being able to speak.

CLITANDRE

Oh, Madame, I would be happy if it were true that you feel all that I feel—and it was permitted for me to judge your soul by mine! But Madame, may I at least believe that it is to you that I owe the thought of this happy stratagem which gives me joy in your presence?

LUCINDA

If you don't owe me the idea, you are at least indebted

to me for having approved the proposition with great joy.

SGANARELLE

(to Lisette) It seems to me he's speaking awfully close to her.

LISETTE

(to Sganarelle) That's so he can observe her physiognomy and all the features of her face.

CLITANDRE

(to Lucinda) Will you be constant, Madame, in all these kindnesses you are showing me?

LUCINDA

But, you—will you be firm in the decisions you've taken?

CLITANDRE

Ah, Madame, until death. I want nothing more than to be with you—and I am going to make it appear in what you are going to see me do.

SGANARELLE

(to Clitandre) Well—our patient? She seems to me a

little brighter.

CLITANDRE

It's that I've already employed on her one of those remedies that my art shows me. As the mind has a great empire over the body—so often illness proceeds from it—my habit is to run to cure the mind before coming to the body—I have observed her looks, the features of her face and the lines of both her hands and through the science heaven has given me, I've recognized that it was the mind which made her ill, and that all her illness comes only from a disordered imagination, from a depraved desire of wanting to be married. As for me, I see nothing more extravagant and more ridiculous than this wish to be married.

SGANARELLE

(aside) Here's a clever man.

CLITANDRE

And I've had—and will have for it, for my entire life—a terrible aversion to it.

SGANARELLE

(aside) Here's a great doctor.

CLITANDRE

But as one must flatter the imagination of patients, and what I've seen in her of alienation of the mind, and even were there not some peril in giving prompt aid—I've taken her through her weakness and told her I've come to ask for her in marriage. Suddenly her face changed—her complexion lit up—her eyes became animated and if you like, for several days to confirm her in this error, you will see it will extract her from where she is.

SGANARELLE

Yeah—I really want that.

CLITANDRE

Later, we will use other remedies to cure her entirely of this fantasy.

SGANARELLE

Yes, that's the best thing in the world. Well! My daughter, here's the gentleman who wants to marry you and I told him I really want that.

LUCINDA

Alas—is it possible?

SGANARELLE

Yes.

LUCINDA

But in good faith?

SGANARELLE

Yes, yes.

LUCINDA

(to Clitandre) What—you feel like being my husband?

CLITANDRE

Yes, Madame.

LUCINDA

And my father consents to it?

SGANARELLE

Yes, my daughter.

LUCINDA

Ah, how happy I would be if that were true.

CLITANDRE

Don't doubt it, Madame. It's not from today that I love you and that I am burning to see myself your husband. I came here only for that—and if you want me to tell you exactly how things stand, this outfit is only an invented pretext and I've only played doctor so as to approach you and obtain what I wish.

LUCINDA

This gives me indeed tender proofs of love and I am as sensible of it as I can be.

SGANARELLE

(aside) Oh—crazy woman—crazy woman—crazy woman.

LUCINDA

Father, do you really intend to give me this gentleman for a spouse?

SGANARELLE

Yes, here—give me your hand. Give me yours a little to see.

CLITANDRE

But, sir.

SGANARELLE

(choking with laughter) No, no, it's to—to satisfy her mind, shake! There that's done.

CLITANDRE

Accept as a proof of my faith this ring, I am giving you. (low to Sganarelle) It's a special ring which cures wandering minds.

LUCINDA

Let's sign the contract so nothing is lacking.

CLITANDRE

Indeed, I really wish it, Madame. (low to Sganarelle) I'm going to bring up the man who writes my prescriptions and make her think he's a notary.

SGANARELLE

Very fine.

CLITANDRE

Hey—bring up the notary I brought with me.

LUCINDA

What! You brought a notary?

CLITANDRE

Yes, Madame.

LUCINDA

I am ravished.

SGANARELLE

Oh—madwoman—oh, madwoman!

(The Notary comes in.)

(Clitandre whispers to the Notary.)

SGANARELLE

(to the Notary) Yes, sir, it's necessary to draw up a contract for these two persons here. Write!

(the Notary writes) Here—let the contract be done. I give her 20,000 shillings in marriage. Write.

LUCINDA

I am much obliged to you, father.

NOTARY

There—it's done—you have only to sign.

SGANARELLE

Here's a contract soon constructed.

CLITANDRE

(to Sganarelle) At least.

SGANARELLE

Hey—no, I tell you.

(to Notary) Come give him the pen to sign.

(to Lucinda) Come on—sign, sign, sign—go, go, I will sign soon enough, myself.

LUCINDA

No, no—I want to have the contract in my hands.

SGANARELLE

Well, here!

(after having signed) Are you satisfied?

LISETTE

More than you can imagine.

CLITANDRE

All the same, I not only took the precaution of bringing a notary—I even brought singers and instruments to celebrate the wedding and rejoice us—have them come—these are the folks I bring with me to pacify troubled minds with their harmonizing.

(Comedy, Ballet and Music enter)

TOGETHER

Without us, all men would become unhealthy—and we—who are their best doctors.

COMEDY

Do you want to chase off—with soft means

Vapors of the spleen who

Then forget Hippocrates

And come to us!

TOGETHER

Without us—all men would become unhealthy—and we—who are their best doctors—

(While they play, Laughter and the Pleasures dance—Clitandre leads Lucinda off.)

SGANARELLE

Here's a pleasant way of curing! Where are the doctor and my daughter?

LISETTE

They want to consummate the marriage.

SGANARELLE

What do you mean, the marriage?

LISETTE

My word, sir—the goose is cooked and what you thought was a game remains a truth.

SGANARELLE

What the devil? (he wants to go after Clitandre and Lucinda but the dancers hold him back) Let me go, let me go, I tell you! (the dancers keep restraining him) Still? (they try to force Sganarelle to dance) Plague on people!

CURTAIN

ABOUT THE AUTHOR

Frank J. Morlock has written and translated many plays since retiring from the legal profession in 1992. His translations have also appeared on Project Gutenberg, the Alexandre Dumas Père web page, Literature in the Age of Napoléon, Infinite Artistries.com, and Munsey's (formerly Blackmask). In 2006 he received an award from the North American Jules Verne Society for his translations of Verne's plays. He lives and works in México.

www.ingramcontent.com/pod-product-compliance
Lightning Source LLC
LaVergne TN
LVHW041615070426
835507LV00008B/256